LAWS ARE BROKEN. RULES GET BENT.

THE A**X**IOMS OF
MARKETING

THE
6 INVARIABLE
PROPOSITIONS
THAT UNDERLIE
AND DETERMINE
EVERY MARKETING
SUCCESS

K
PUBLISHING

ROBERT W. BLY

www. **K**ALLISTIpublishing.com

ISBN-13 978-1-7359792-1-2

Library of Congress Control Number: 2020949217

DESIGNED & PRINTED IN THE UNITED STATES OF AMERICA

CONTENTS

This book is for James Lange.

ACKNOWLEDGMENTS

Thanks to my publisher, Anthony Raymond Michalski, for having faith in me and this book, his long patience waiting for it to get to his desk, and his boundless enthusiasm, energy, and ideas. Thanks also to all the marketers who contributed stories, ideas, case studies, and samples of their promotions. For privacy, I use your initials and not your full name throughout the book. I would also like to thank Roy Furr for his contributions to chapter one.

Some sections of the book appeared, in slightly different form, in DM News and Target Marketing. Also note that some of the ideas in the Fourth Axiom were first articulated by veteran marketer Ed Nash in his book **Direct Marketing: Strategy, Planning, Execution: Fourth Edition** *(McGraw-Hill, 2000, pp. 153-154).*

"*A book that instructs in some profitable field is a priceless treasure. It never forgets even a minor principle of its conceptual message, yet it will not scold you if you forget even the major ones. It will not rebuke you for your tardiness or slow-witted comprehension. Such a book ranks as one of man's best friends. And if the bookseller offers i t a nd you fail t o a ssume ownership, w ho w ill b e t he poorer, you o r he?*"
—*Jerry Buchanan, Towers Club USA Newsletter, #39*

FOREWORD

I don't know if a marketing book can give you a Junior MBA just from its Table Of Contents — but if such a thing were possible, this would the first book to pack that much punch. You should make the Table Of Contents page an object of serious study.

Many a highly-paid Wharton MBA has made the mistakes listed in this book. Then made them again.

In the introduction, Bob Bly offers a dictionary definition of an *AXIOM*. Here's mine:

> *Axioms are the deep truths (or assumptions) that run everything in your life. They work whether you're aware of them or not. And since most people are NOT aware of their assumptions, they are unable to question them.*

Sergey Brin questioned how we rank science papers and Google was born.

Travis Kalanick questioned taxi dispatching and Über was born.

Fred Smith questioned the structure of the shipping industry and FedEx was born.

Steve Jobs asked what a telephone could become and the iPhone was born.

This is not a book about questioning assumptions and shattering paradigms. Rather, this is a book about mastering the basics first ... so you can get to the REAL questions.

Brian Kurtz likes to say, "Learn the rules like a pro so you can break them like an artist."

Most entrepreneurs have great contributions to make, but

never make them because they're so stressed from meeting their monthly obligations, they never get to the great discoveries.

This book will cover your monthly obligations with solid blocking and tackling so your bills are always paid. Freeing you to innovate and focus on the real problems of the world. Ever cut open an avocado and let it sit? A day later it's black. Most marketing education (especially online) is like that avocado. Avocados spoil in hours; many marketing educations are just as rotten in six months.

Marketers are suckers for this. Because they're so chronically obsessed with the latest techniques (search engine fads, ways of gaming the system, short-term promos, scrambles for fast cash) they reward teachers for feeding them this stuff.

Principles are different. If you know deep principles, you don't need to memorize a huge list of constantly-changing methods and techniques. This book is about the soundest principles of direct marketing. They were valid before fax machines were invented, and they'll still work in the future, after the Internet is unrecognizable compared to what it is today.

The first step to being a great innovator is figuring out what rules you are allowed to break and which ones you can't. Bob's Axioms are the things that will NOT change, the rules you can't break.

That's why you need to read this book.*

In a world of fake news and echo chambers and "post truth" (which was the 2016 International Word Of The Year, accord-

---

* The "Marketing Rules of Thumb" sidebar in Bob's introduction is worth the price of admission all by itself.

ing to *Oxford English Dictionary*) I am heartened by the fact that marketers of all people are returning to first principles. You're picking up books like this one. Is a new renaissance perhaps underway?

Are You Tired of the "New Bag Of Tricks" Treadmill Yet? Maybe it's time to get off. This book's your exit ramp.

Perry Marshall
Chicago, IL

Perry Marshall is the author of *80/20 Sales & Marketing*, *Ultimate Guide to Google Adwords*, *Ultimate Guide to Facebook Advertising*, and *Evolution 2.0*.

INTRODUCTION

There are some subjects in which seemingly every one — or at least a whole lot of people — think they are experts. Marketing is one of these topics.

There are two reasons why everyone is a "marketing expert." The first is: marketing is not a technical subject, like astrophysics or small engine repair. Therefore, people believe they can learn it or already know it; two other topics or skills that vast hordes of people believe they know or can do well because these areas are also not technical are photography and writing. Everyone thinks they can take a great picture. Everyone writes. And almost everyone thinks they know what works in marketing.

Second, almost everybody in business is a marketer, at least part of the time. Their primary job function may be sales, operations, manufacturing, R&D, engineering, or finance. But sooner or later their opinion will be sought on a marketing campaign or promotion.*

Amateurs tend to base their critiques of marketing programs mainly on subjective judgment, while marketing professionals follow a body of knowledge or set of rules. The problem is that a lot of marketing "rules" arise out of false pretenses, erroneous conclusions, or simple lack of understanding. Yet marketers accept these flimsy rules as the gospel.

---

* With all these amateurs running interference on our campaigns as if they know that they are doing, no wonder so many marketers become disgruntled with the profession from time to time. In fact, 47% of advertising industry employees surveyed in 2016 by *Campaign* rated their morale as low, and 63% of them were job hunting!

For example, a marketer does a mailing with a blue postcard and it generates 20% greater response than his white postcard. The marketer tells this story to colleagues or perhaps in front of a crowd at a marketing meeting. Then one of the listeners brings the story back to her office, where she tells the boss that she learned a new rule of direct marketing: blue out-pulls white by 20 percent. The marketer who did the original test writes an article about it for a trade journal. Before you know it, "blue out-pulls white" has become a commandment – based on one single test.

Of course, that isn't a rule at all. It's an observation based on a single mailing. We don't know whether enough postcards were mailed to give us a statistically valid test. We don't even know whether there was any variation in postcard copy or design save the color, so the validity of the result is even more in question.

Take a look at the infographic in Fig. I-1. These are marketing "rules of thumb" based on long experience and observation. But they are just that: rules of thumb. They are accurate a lot of the time, even most of the time. But not all of the time. There is nothing inherent in them that says they always have to be true. And they sometimes are not.

The main point though is: you can't formulate a rule based on a single test result. For something to be a rule, it must be observed to be true in marketing over an extended period in multiple circumstances.

There is no rule today in direct mail that says blue postcards always out-pull white postcards. But there are rules in many areas of marketing. For instance, we know that when we put large

"order now" buttons on web pages, we get more sales than when we just underline and hyperlink the words "order now" or use a hyperlinked URL in the text.

The *Compact Oxford English Dictionary* defines rules as "a broadly accurate guide or principle, based on practice rather than on theory." In direct mail, there is a rule that says if you repeat a direct mail promotion a few weeks after you first mail it, the second mailing will generate approximately half the response of the first mailing to the same list. But does that mean it is a certainty on a par with the certainty that the sun will rise tomorrow morning?

There are plenty of rules in marketing, so when Anthony Raymond Michalski of Kallisti Publishing asked me to write a book of marketing rules, I readily agreed. Then he dropped the hammer: "What I want is a book of the most important marketing axioms, not just rules."

I ran back to the *Compact Oxford English Dictionary* which told me that an axiom is "a proposition regarded as self-evidently true." What's the difference between a rule and an axiom? A rule is a guideline to follow that has a strong probability of yielding the expected result. An axiom is an immutable law which can be violated only under the most extraordinary circumstances, if at all.

"The real substance of our universe, and thus of life itself, is comprised of universal principles," says best-selling author Robert Ringer. "These universal principles, also known as axioms, truths, or natural laws, form the infrastructure for the stage of life on which each of us performs."

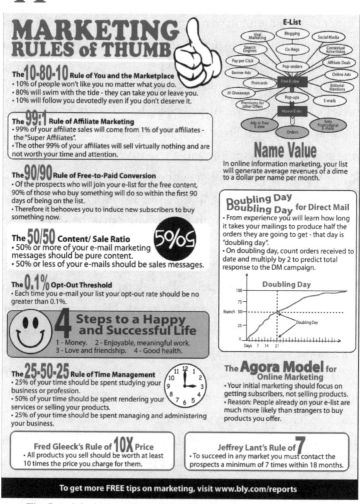

Fig. I-1. Marketing rules of thumb.

Let me give you my favorite example of an axiom. I have written in my weekly e-newsletter, *The Direct Response Letter*, that multi-tasking does not work, citing multiple psychological studies showing that people are 40 percent less productive when they multitask.

Those studies, while persuasive, support my no-multitasking rule. But unassailable logic elevates the principle that multitasking does not work to an axiom. The logic is simple and beyond dispute: if you are doing two tasks at one time, than it is axiomatic that neither of them is getting your full attention. Therefore it is an axiom, not just a rule, that multi-tasking diminishes effectiveness.

Were there any axioms of marketing, let alone one? Or were all marketing principles rules only? I embarked on a research project, which include a survey of my 65,000 e-newsletter subscribers, to find out. The answers are in the pages that follow.

In this book you have the undeniable truths about marketing, what it can do, and how it works. Perhaps you have already discovered these axioms and proven them to yourself. Some you may not have encountered or become aware of. But whatever the case, one thing is certain: you ignore them at your peril. They work virtually all the time, and when you defy these axioms, your marketing results invariably falls short of the mark.

The value of having these axioms written out for you is, I think, obvious, but in case not, let me state it plainly: By obeying these axioms, and making your promotions conform to them, you can substantially improve your marketing results. Conversely, when you ignore all or even one of these marketing axioms, you do so at your peril, risking poor results and monetary losses.

I realize that declaring the principles in this book to be axioms is a slippery slope. And you may question whether these are truly axioms or instead mere rules, guidelines, or principles. What's most important is not their descriptor but that these axi-

oms really can and do hold true throughput the sphere of marketing activity — from social media and mobile marketing to search engine optimization and e-mail.

One other advantage of mastering and following these axioms of marketing is that they, unlike marketing technology and channels, are immutable and do not change over time. "The same principles of human desire and methods of influence that guided the markets of ancient Greece are still operating today," write Craig Simpson and Brian Kurtz in their book *The Advertising Solution* (Entrepreneur Press, 2016, p. xviii). "In order to get people to do what you want them to do, you have to understand what motivates them. You also have to know how to present yourself and your product to get their interest, their trust, and ultimately their willingness to call you, visit you, or send you their money." Or as Claude Hopkins observed, "Human psychology has not changed in ten centuries."

I do have a favor to ask. If you have discovered marketing axioms other than the ones described here, or dispute any of them, or have new evidence to support them, please send them to me so I can share them with readers of the next edition. Contact me here:

Bob Bly

Copywriter

www.bly.com

31 Cheyenne Drive • Montville, NJ 07045

Phone 973-263-0562 • Fax 931-263-0613

rwbly@bly.com

A**X**IOM™ ¹
OF MARKETING

MARKETING EFFECTIVENESS IS NOT SUBJECTIVE

Measuring and Testing Are the Only Ways to Definitively Know What Works in Your Marketing

MARKETING EFFECTIVENESS IS NOT SUBJECTIVE

Ken Weissman, who ran a small graphic design study in New Jersey, once told me "Subjective judgment is the death of the service business." But almost everyone in marketing knows that his activities are invariably going to be commented upon and evaluated by one or more reviewers relying largely on subjective perception.

In a large corporation, it's a fact of life that creating marketing campaigns is a team sport. Even in small businesses, there may be a lively debate about graphics, list, or copy between the company owner, his sales VP, their marketing agency, and perhaps the chief engineer who thinks everyone in marketing is an idiot.

The problem with subjective judgment is that it is opinion, and opinion is not fact. Worse, when everyone seems to have an opinion, who is to say whose opinion is right?

In the early 1980s, I was the advertising manager for Koch Engineering, a manufacturer of process equipment for the oil and gas, chemical, and other process industries. My boss reported directly to the company president, David Koch, better known today as half of the billionaire Koch brothers. But David, who has passed away, was much less famous when I worked for him decades ago, although at the time he was running for vice president of the United States of America on the Libertarian party ticket.

In a meeting, a group of us were debating the merits of a proposed redesign of our 40-foot trade show exhibit. Suddenly, David's voice boomed out: "Do you know what a cow is?" We were shocked into silence. What was he talking about? David paused, then said, "A cow is a moose designed by committee."

Some businesspeople believe that you should ask as many people as possible for their opinion of your proposed promotion because you never know who will have a good suggestion. David did not, as far as I could see, believe this, and neither do I. As the old expression notes, opinions are like rear-ends: everyone has one.

Subjective judgment will perhaps never be eliminating from the marketing process. Yes, with the move toward digital marketing, results can be measured more quickly and easily than ever before. But before a landing page ever gets posted or an e-mail message distributed, someone has to give it his or her OK based mainly on opinion.

Writes Laura Lowell in *42 Rules of Marketing: Second Edition* (Superstar Press):

> *When you are a marketer, everyone thinks they can do your job better than you. Everyone from your spouse, friends, colleague and even the folks at your local coffee shop — they all have opinions on your latest marketing campaign. 'I would have…' 'Why didn't you…?' 'I don't get it.'"*
>
> *What other professions can you think of where everyone gets to tell you how to do your job? You don't tell the engineers how to solve technical problems. You don't tell doctors how to diagnose an illness. You wouldn't tell a lawyer how to prosecute their case. Yet engineers, doctors and lawyers feel like they can tell how you should have done your latest TV ad."*

There are two problems related to making marketing decisions based on subjective opinion. The first is that subjective judgment is a guess, and virtually everyone guesses incorrectly about virtually everything, at least part of the time. "Will it rain today? Should I ask my boss for a raise now or wait until a better time? Will the seller accept my bid or will she think it is too high and I won't get the house?" We don't know. We can only guess, and we are frequently wrong.

The second problem is that business in general and marketing in particular are counter-intuitive: what works is frequently the opposite of what people think will work. For instance, I often pose this question in my marketing seminar: "If someone donates to your nonprofit, when should you send your next fundraising solicitation to him?" Common answers include: next year ... in a few months ... in a month.

The correct answer is: the day you get his donation. My students are amazed when they hear it and object that this makes no sense. Their reasoning: if Fred just sent a donation, he doesn't have money to send another.

Sounds logical ... perhaps. But it is wrong. The axiom of RFM, or Recency Frequency Monetary — which we cover in Axiom #3 — proves irrefutably this sub-axiom of marketing: *the customer who just purchased is the one most likely to purchase again.* The more recently a donor has sent a contribution, the more likely they are to do so again. If Fred just gave to your cause, it's at the top of his mind, and he is in the mood to help right now. So let him by asking for another donation. Counterintuitive, but countless tests prove it true.

MEASUREMENT TRUMPS SUBJECTIVE JUDGMENT

The biggest flaw of subjective judgment is that it does not have a metric by which its validity can be measured. I am in complete

agreement with Lord Kelvin, inventor of the Kelvin tempera-
ture scale, in which zero is absolute zero, who said: "When you
can measure and express something in numbers, then you know
something about it." It is a great mantra for scientists like Kelvin, engineers like me and David Koch, and marketers.

People who give their subjective opinions virtually never
back them up with metrics. Their opinions are gut feel, not quan-
tifiable, and therefore of extremely limited validity and value.

"'Seat of the pants' guesswork is old-fashioned and ama-
teurish," wrote the late copywriter Herschel Gordon Lewis in an
article in *Today@TargetMarketing* (9/21/2016). He advised that
marketers should always test, and failure to test is naïve on any
marketer's part.

"Accept nothing as true about advertising until you've tested
it yourself," writes Craig Simpson in his book *The Advertising Solution* (Entrepreneur Press, 2016, p. 164). "Every new ad is a test of
what worked before. Constantly check results — measured, as
always, by response rates — to see what is working. Be willing to
scrap something you might have loved if something else proves
to be better."

I recently read a Facebook post in which MS, a social media
evangelist, asked, "Does anyone know who is crushing it on In-
stagram these days?"

I commented: "What do you mean by crushing it?" No one
on the thread answered with anything close to a measurable
metric such as views or click-through or conversions. What they
mean by "crushing it" — a phrase I despise, by the way, because it's boastful — is that they created a really cool-looking

infographic. My immediate response: So what? To quote an old saying, that and a dime will get you a cup of coffee.

Here's how you identify an Internet marketer who knows that subjective judgment means squat and the only way to measure marketing is by the metrics. Look for the guy (or gal) running around the office, collecting numbers from the sales staff. What's he asking?

> "How many calls are coming in?"
> "What promo are the callers mentioning when they call?"
> "What is their reaction to the bonus? The offer?"
> "What's working better — package one or package two?"
> "What list is working better — list one or list two?"

Or they're sitting at their computer, constantly checking their online orders for promo codes. Constantly keeping up with the Google ads stats. Pressing the pedal to the metal on Google Analytics. Constantly looking at where their web site traffic is coming from and how the different traffic sources convert into customers.

Notice nowhere did I say they're leaning back in their genius chair, pondering how to get people to respond. Sure, they may do that on occasion. But what separates the wheat from the chaff is analyzing results. And with that, testing.

TEST TO IMPROVE RESULTS

If you want to be an Internet marketing genius, you test. If you're fine just blending into the crowd of marketing mediocrity, you don't test.

Test. Test. Test. It's the single most important thing you can do to become an Internet marketing genius.

This is not a new concept. One of the classic books of advertising wisdom is a book called *Scientific Advertising* by Claude Hopkins. From the first chapter of his book:

> *The time has come when advertising has in some hands reached the status of a science. It is based on fixed principles and is reasonably exact. The causes and effects have been analyzed until they are well understood. The correct methods of procedure have been proved and established. We know what is most effective, and we act on basic law.*
>
> *Advertising, once a gamble, has thus become, under able direction, one of the safest business ventures. Certainly no other enterprise with comparable possibilities need involve so little risk...*
>
> *We learn the principles and prove them by repeated tests. This is done through keyed advertising, by traced returns, largely by the use of coupons. We compare one way with many others, backward and forward, and record the results. When one method invariably proves best, that method becomes a fixed principle.*

Scientific Advertising was written in 1923. The advertising wisdom in it still holds true today.* What we learned from Hopkins was that by testing various approaches, we can take most of the guesswork out of advertising, including Internet marketing. We can make big profits more of a sure thing by applying what worked before. And we can prepare ourselves for future success by tracking our results and reusing what has been successful.

---

* If you haven't read it yet, you should. The knowledge you'll gain by reading this chapter on modern testing methods will be greatly enhanced by reading or re-reading Hopkins' classic.

MARKETING EFFECTIVENESS IS NOT SUBJECTIVE

Most importantly, we shouldn't rely on our own creativity to come up with the best, most effective method of trying to market our products or services. We should test!

And where we have Hopkins beat hands down is we have far more advanced methods for testing our online marketing than he could ever dream of.

Recently I learned about a study done by QualPro, a company that runs a large number of tests on both manufacturing and marketing. They analyzed 14,000 tests they had been a part of over 20 years. What they found is interesting. They tested 14,000 different variables against their control promotions. A "control" is the best-performing ad you are currently running. The whole point of testing is to create a new promotion that outperforms the control.

The results of the study showed that out of 14,000 things tested:

> 53% had little to no effect on results, as compared to the control.

> 22% of the things tested actually made things worse.

> Only 25% — 1 in 4 — actually improved the manufacturing process or advertisement.

And these tests were designed by experts! Why make changes based on what you think is right when 75% of the time what you think will either decrease response or have no effect at all? Why not test in small quantities so you can quickly identify what it takes to get the optimum response from each marketing campaign?

That's how you'll make the most profit from the least

amount of work, with the least amount of risk — and how you'll soon be known as an Internet marketing genius!

So, I've kind of hammered it in: you need to test. But even with this knowledge many people find excuses not to. They're too busy doing what needs to happen from day to day. They're doing this or they're doing that. They don't know how. I've fallen victim to those excuses too — so I'm not immune. But you won't see results until you start!

So that's why I'm spending so much time emphasizing that you need to apply this knowledge — before I even give it to you. Maybe 50% of the people who read this book will make it a priority to test. Around 25% will follow through and try to set up their first test. Some 10% or so actually will. And a mere 2% will continue testing beyond the first test — even if the other 8% who tries testing gets a big bump to their profits from their first test!

You can give yourself a serious competitive advantage if you just try — and then stick to it.

One of the many direct marketing superstars who believes in extensive testing is Joseph Sugarman, founder of JS&A. The company has sold millions of electronic gadgets plus a slew of BluBlocker sunglasses.

When asked the reason for his great success in marketing, Joe replied,

> *The key was testing. Out of ten products I tested, very often only a few were winners. In fact, I had so many more failures than winners. Direct marketing is often counter-intuitive. What you think works often doesn't, and what you think shouldn't work does. The key is testing*

> *I have had more failures than you could imagine. If I ran a test and it failed chances are the product would not succeed even if I tweaked it. Product is king and your tests are simply to figure out which ones work and which ones don't and to focus on your winners and discard those losers.*

The dumbest trend in today's era of digital marketing is to set as objectives achievements that cannot be measured quantitatively and therefore cannot be accurately tested. For instance, I received an invitation to attend a talk promising to show attendees how to "Build excitement about your brand through live storytelling on Snapchat."

I wrote to the program sponsor and asked whether the speaker would explain how we marketers could measure "excitement" in a way that shows whether these exciting Snapchat storytelling sessions contribute to the bottom line or are an utter waste of time. I am still awaiting a response.

YOU NEED TO KNOW WHAT YOU DON'T KNOW

In marketing, the most important thing is to know what you do not know. And what you do not know is what will work best — whether an offer, a headline, a price point, a new product, or a mailing list — until you test it.

For instance, one of my industrial clients wanted to run banner ads inviting prospects to visit their booth at a trade show. The client was thinking of offering a gift card, which was prompted by a competitor's banner ad offering free movie tickets as the bribe to get the customer into the booth. She was considering a Starbucks gift card vs. an Amazon gift card.

A𝗑IOM 1

"Which would work better?" she asked. I had to answer truthfully: While we could certainly make an educated guess, in fact we would have no idea which works better until and unless we tested one vs. the other.

One of us thought Starbucks was the obvious choice because "Americans are crazy about coffee" today. Another voted for Amazon because "you can get almost anything you want there."

But all of this is mere supposition. Which is really going to bring in more traffic to the trade show booth, Starbucks or Amazon? The only way to know — I repeat, the only way to know — is by testing. There is no other certain method of finding which is gift card is the strongest offer.

We also questioned whether we should specify the dollar amount on the gift cards or not say. Several people said not to mention what the gift was at all and instead to offer a surprise mystery gift.

My client asked me, "Which approach will work best — giving the dollar amount or leaving it out?" I could not answer, because there is no axiom saying that Starbucks beats Amazon gift cards as premiums, or whether saying the card is for $25 would increase or decrease response, or have no effect.

The only axiom is that you do not know what will work best until and unless you test. If that is the only thing you take away from this book after reading it, you will have paid back your investment in it a hundredfold or more, I assure you.

A/B SPLIT TESTING

The classic testing method in direct response is A/B split testing.

You create two versions of your promotion, A and B. Then you run both of them simultaneously. They must run side by side in the same time frame. You cannot run A on Tuesday and B on Friday. Why not? Day of week and what is happening in the news that day can affect the response rate. For instance, a client of mine prepared a direct mail package to sell an investment newsletter. The outer envelope proclaimed in large, bold letters, "Bull market ahead; Dow to soar!" The day it mailed, the stock market crashed and the Dow dropped more than 20% within a few days, and the mailing bombed.

The humbling thing about doing an A/B split test is that, when you try to predict which test cell, A or B, will be the winner, you are so often wrong. It's a powerful lesson to discover that subjective judgment, which seems to drive most of the advertising created by Madison Avenue ad agencies, counts for squat.

In addition, without split testing, you miss out on improvements that could increase your response. I have seen subject line A generate 25% greater click-through rate than subject line B. In direct mail, sales copy A beat sales copy B by 40% in one test. In another, offer A generated 10 times the sales of offer B. And these are not rarities: testing produces dramatic increases in results on a regular basis. Therefore, marketers who do not test are making a foolish error.

According to Marketo's e-book *The Power of A/B Testing*, "A/B testing, also known as split testing, is an efficient and cost-effective marketing strategy that companies cannot, and should not, live without. By trying out different combinations for a specific group of customers, marketers can eliminate elements that alienate users, drive people away, or have no effect on co conversion rates whatsoever."

MarketingSherpa reports that A/B testing can help raise conversion rates by 48% or more. In my own A/B tests for my products and my clients, I have seen a change in just the wording of the offer alone produce an increase in response as much as tenfold, as amazing as that sounds.

There are two approaches to A/B split testing. The first and preferred method is, when testing a promotion, which I call incremental A/B split testing, is to vary only one element between the two versions. For instance, A/B split tests I have been involved in include testing:

> One price vs. another price.

> Color of order button on landing page.

> Photo on landing page.

> Headline A vs. headline B.

> Outer envelope teaser in direct mail package vs. no outer envelope teaser.

> Personalized letter vs. non-personalized letter.

> Direct mail package with brochure and without brochure.

> 10-day money back guarantee vs. 30-day vs. 90-day.

> Offer wording; e.g., "50% discount" vs. "half-off."

> One up-front payment covering the full cost of the product vs. monthly payments.

> Magalog vs. #10 direct mail package.

> One-page sales letter vs. postcard.

> Information premium vs. merchandise premium.

> With vs. without a 3D object enclosed in the envelope.

And that's just the tip of the iceberg. So why do a lot of us old-time direct marketers prefer varying just one element between the A and B test cells?

Because that way, we learn what specifically matters and affects response vs. what variables make no difference. And we can apply the lessons learned to many other campaigns. For instance, if testing proves that red type in a landing page headline outpulls blue in test after test, we will make it standard practice to use red instead of blue. Testing one element helps us hone in on what works best for our offer in our market — priceless knowledge without which you are creating advertising in the dark.

The second school of testing says to test two completely different versions of your promotion. Not just a single elements is varied; the two promotions may have different copy, design, format, and offer. The advantage of this approach is that it can potentially produce a dramatic increase in response rates. The drawback is that you do not know what caused the increase in response. Was it the whole package? Just headline? The color? A/B split testing of only one variable helps you learn what works best in your marketing — for instance, that orange click buttons on your landing pages generate more clicks than red, yellow, or green.

HOW MANY PIECES MUST YOU TEST?

The question I am most often asked about testing direct mail is: how many pieces must I test to get a statistically valid test result?

The answer of course is based on statistics. I do not understand the reason why the statistics I am about to give you are accurate, because I am not a statistician. But I know for a fact, through decades of testing, that they are accurate.

To begin with, the statistical validity of a test is not really based on how many messages you mail, e-mail, or post but on how many responses you get. To illustrate, if you need 20 responses to get a statistically valid test result, and your response rates are typically one percent, then you would have to mail 2,000 pieces per test cell.

Note that I said per test cell, not total. The statistical validity calculations apply to each individual test cell, not the whole mailing. So if you have two test cells, A and B, you would have to, in the above scenario, mail 2,000 pieces in each test cell, or 4,000 total. The table below is used to determine the number of pieces you must mail per test cell to get a statistically valid result. The two variables in the table are confidence level and deviation of decline percent.

Confidence level refers to how certain you can be that the results of your test are valid. If you mail enough pieces to achieve a 99% confidence level, you are almost certain that your test results can be trust.

Determining Test–Cell Size: The Number of Returns Required for a Statistically Valid Test

Confidence Level	Deviation or Decline Percent*			
	50%	25%	12.5%	6.25%
75%	1.8	7.3	29.2	116.8
85%	3.5	14.0	56.0	
90%	6.6	26.2	104.8	
95%	11.0	42.8		
99%	21.7	86.9		

*The estimated return and your break-even point or the decline percent you wish to protect yourself against.

MARKETING EFFECTIVENESS IS NOT SUBJECTIVE

Deviation or decline percent refers to how much lower the response rate on the full mailing will be than the test. A 25% decline percentage means that if the test generated a 2% response, the roll-out — mailing a larger volume of the direct mail package following the test — will likely produce a response rate of no less than 1.5%, which is a 25% decline from 2%.

Let's say the mailing list has 100,000 names and you test 2,000 names. For the roll-out to hold to the confidence level and decline percent predicted by the table, it can't be more than 10-times the size of the test. So after the test, we would mail 20,000 names, not the whole list.

The roll-out to the 20,000 names will generate a certain response, likely between 1.5% and 2%. Now you can roll out again to the remainder of the list, which is 80,000 names, confident that again you will get a similar response.

Before you mail, you have to make the decision of what confidence level and percent decline is acceptable to you. My personal preference is an 85% confidence level with a 25% decline. That means I can be 85% certain that my roll out results won't be less than 25% below the test results I get.

If we circle each of these rows and columns (see below), they intersect at 14. This means we need to mail enough pieces to get 14 responses in order for our test to have a 25% decline rate with an 85% confidence level. If we anticipate a 1% response rate, that means each test cell — A and B — must mail 1,400 names apiece. Since we are guessing at the anticipated response rate, in this situation I would make each test cell 2,000 names, for a total test mailing of 4,000 names.

Let's say you wanted more certainty in the statistical validity of your test. If you picked a 90% confidence level with only a 12.5% decline, you would need, given an estimated one percent response rate, to mail around 10,000 pieces per test cell. That's too rich for my blood, and I'm happier doing 2,000 pieces per test cell in exchange for a slightly lower confidence level and slightly larger decline percent.

Determining Test–Cell Size: The Number of Returns Required for a Statistically Valid Test

| Confidence Level | Deviation or Decline Percent* | | | |
	50%	25%	12.5%	6.25%
75%	1.8	7.3	29.2	116.8
85%	3.5	14.0	56.0	
90%	6.6	26.2	104.8	
95%	11.0	42.8		
99%	21.7	86.9		

The estimated return and your break-even point or the decline percent you wish to protect yourself against.

Yes, you can do a much smaller test — as few as a couple of hundred names — and get a rough feel for whether your promotion is working. But those results are not statistically valid, and therefore you should be cautious about expanding a campaign based on such a small test. If you want to roll out with greater confidence, test the number of pieces indicated by the table above.

One big name in direct response told me I was stupid for settling for a mere 85% confidence level and 25% decline; his agency preferred 95% confidence and 12.5% decline, which he said made them more comfortable predicting response to their roll-outs. But another direct marketer, a list broker who conducted thousands of tests for his clients over a period of decades, said his experience matched what the statistical table on the previous page indicates: 2,000 names per test cell is enough to base a roll-out decision on.

How to decide which is for you? Use test grids.

TEST GRIDS

So let's say that, using the above statistical analysis, you determine you need to mail 2,000 pieces to get a statistically valid test.

You want to test three prices — $49, $99, and $149. But you also want to test three different outer envelope teasers — A, B, and C. You in fact can test all these variables at once by creating a test grid with 9 different test cells as follows:

Price: Teaser:	$49	$99	$149
A	2,000	2,000	2,000
B	2,000	2,000	2,000
C	2,000	2,000	2,000

In this way, with a mailing of only 18,000 pieces, we can test three price points and three envelope teasers all at the same time, and get a statistically valid answer as to which price as well as which teaser produces the best results.

TAGUCHI TESTING

Taguchi testing, also called multivariate testing, uses the speed and power of the Internet to go way beyond traditional split testing and test many more variables simultaneously. Let's see how that can work.

To begin with, if you want to make a lot of money in Internet marketing, you have to learn two things: traffic (how to drive visitors to your site) and conversion.

Taguchi testing measures how you convert a maximum percentage of your web traffic to paid customers. Most marketers just put up a landing page, and whatever the conversion is, that's it. They may occasionally try a different headline or split test a new landing page. But that's infrequent.

What they don't recognize is focusing on half of the equation only gets you a fraction of the results. The most successful marketers focus on both traffic and conversion, increasing both at the same time to create exponential growth in sales and profits. Taguchi testing is perhaps the most powerful method in use today for increasing the conversions of your Internet marketing.

With Taguchi testing you can quickly, affordably, and easily increase your landing page conversion rates by 25% to 200% or more — doubling or even tripling your conversions, sales, and profits. If you're familiar with split testing (A/B testing), you may wonder how Taguchi testing is different. Here's the short answer.

As discussed, split testing (A/B testing) lets you to test different variations of one part of your advertisement, web site, or landing page against one another. The next step beyond split testing is **multivariate testing** (MVT) — which just means testing more than one variable at a time.

Taguchi testing is a form of MVT that uses statistics to leverage your testing — with Taguchi you only have to test a fraction of the total number of possible combinations of variables to understand how all possible combinations would perform. This will make a lot more sense as we go on.

Split testing started as a way to increase the effectiveness of off-line advertising. You could test multiple headlines against one another. Or multiple order forms. Or any other part of your advertisement or direct mail piece.

But split testing has traditionally been limited to two variations of a single element. You tested only the headline. Or only the order form. You were limited. It took weeks or months to get results. And it was expensive because you'd run test after test to optimize the complete ad!

Taguchi's big benefit over traditional split testing and even MVT is that you can test a small number of combinations to understand how all possible combinations would perform. This means you can test just 12 landing pages to learn how 2,048 landing page variations would perform, or 18 to learn how 4,374 would perform.

Once you run your Taguchi test, you'll learn which combination results in the best performing landing page — not out of the 12 or 18 you tested directly, but out of the 2,048 or 4,374 total combinations possible. It also tells you which variables made a difference, how big of a difference they made, and which was the most effective. (This is valuable information for future tests!)

Thanks to the Internet and new Taguchi software, you can run these tests quickly, cheaply, and easily. This ensures you're converting as many of your page visitors into paid customers as possible, shifting your journey to online marketing success to warp speed. And it gives you huge advantages you wouldn't have if you had to test variation against variation, element by element, using traditional A/B split testing.

Taguchi and MVT have been featured by *Forbes Magazine*, The *Wall Street Journal*, *Inc. Magazine*, *Business Week*, The *New York Times*, *Advertising Age*, *Marketing Sherpa*, *MarketingProfs.com*, *MarketingExperiments. com*, *Quality Magazine*, and tons of other renowned publications.*

The *Wall Street Journal* featured a case study with Lowe's: "Many advertising decisions boil down to someone's hunch about what might work best. Lowe's, the nation's second largest home-improvement retailer, says it has found a way to eliminate some of that guesswork."

Inc. Magazine says, "It's a bloody miracle. [It] not only shows the right way to do something, it also tells you what the cost in dollars will be of doing it the wrong way." *Advertising Age* called it a "breakthrough methodology."

With Taguchi testing, you can improve conversions by 25% to 300% or more on your website — increasing profits without spending more on sending traffic to your website. And how by continuous testing of your landing pages, you could easily stumble on a situation where you create a 1,000% or 2,000% increase in sales conversions in just a couple of weeks. In fact, it could even happen in your first test!

What this means is if you have a web page converting 1% of visitors right now, soon you could be converting $1\frac{1}{4}$%, $4\frac{1}{2}$%, or even as much as 10% of visitors. This can happen in a matter of weeks — not months or years — and usually doesn't require you to significantly increase the amount of money you spend to drive people to your website.

The bad news is that Taguchi testing is a complicated sub-

---

* Plus on too many websites to count.

ject, and so teaching you how to do it is beyond the scope of this chapter or this book.*

---

*If you want to master Taguchi testing, I recommend *The Taguchi Testing Handbook* by Roy Furr, which I published as an e-book and is available at _http://www.taguchitestinghandbook.com/_.

A$\overset{2}{X}$IOM™
OF MARKETING

LIKEABILITY ‡ EFFECTIVENESS

There is No Correlation Between
Advertisement's Likeability and Its
Effectiveness

Notice first that we said there is no correlation between people *liking* an ad and being *persuaded* by the ad. But by "ad likeability," we mean people *liking the ad as an object in itself:* finding it funny, clever, entertaining, moving, or exciting. A huge error in marketing is to focus on the ad as entertainment or "art." Doing so reminds the prospect, "This is an ad you are looking at, and we are trying to sell you something." Most people don't like being sold, and so the ad instantly loses effectiveness.

Another form of likeability is "product likeability." If the ad makes the consumer like the product, and not the ad itself, then the prospect indeed becomes more inclined to buy.

However, advertising that people like wins awards, the most famous being the coveted Clio Award for best TV commercial. But do all those funny and clever award-winning commercials and ads win sales? In this chapter, you get the surprising answer — namely that, contrary to intuition, there is no correlation between people liking or being entertained by a commercial or ad and the product sales generated by that commercial or ad.

For example, one of my favorite pieces of short film in the last few years was the Budweiser Clydesdale commercial broadcast during the Super Bowl. It tells the story of a horse breeder who forms an emotional attachment with one of the Clydesdales he raises from a foal; when grown, the horse is sold to Budweiser to work pulling a beer wagon in parades and such.

One day, the horse breeder sees that the Budweiser wagon pulled by his horse will be featured in a parade in the nearest city. He goes to get a glimpse of the horse, for whom he still feels an attachment. But the horse has blinders on, blocking its side vision. So it doesn't see the man as it goes by. A bit dejected and sad, he heads toward his parked car. Meanwhile, the parade over, the blinders are removed from the horse who immediately sees the human who lovingly raised him. The horse breaks free and gallops full speed through the Chicago streets. The horse breeder sees the horse in his side mirror, gets out of the car, and as the horse comes to him, it stops and he fondly embraces the animal in a sentimental tear-jerker of a reunion.

In sixty seconds this short film tells, with no dialogue, a powerful emotional tale of affection between a human and an animal. But while it succeeds as a film, is it a success as a commercial?

BUT DOES IT SELL?

Unfortunately not, and largely because of the Second Axiom of marketing, which states that *there is no correlation between an advertisement being entertaining, clever, funny, or creative and it being effective, effectiveness being measured by response or sales.*

In addition, it's common with the more entertaining commercials that people cannot recall the product that was advertised, even shortly after watching the spot.

In none of the write-ups in the trade press following the Super Bowl that praised this commercial did I read anything about its sales, and that is because many professionals in brand, image, and general advertising — as well as the majority of the general public — judge advertising not on effectiveness (*i.e.*, sales) but on something else: entertainment value. In other words, by how funny, clever, dramatic, entertaining, or moving it is.

A study by an ad-testing firm found that while funny TV commercials get more attention and are better liked, funniness had little correlation with effectiveness in a scoring system that measured watchability and persuasion, among other factors. In fact, funny ads were slightly less likely to increase desire or purchase intent than unfunny ones.

An article in *Harvard Business Review* (June, 2013) notes,

> *There's no firm evidence that shows how (creative) messages influence purchase behavior. Similarly, there is remarkably little empirical research that ties creative messaging to actual sales revenues … because brand managers have lacked a systematic way to assets the effectiveness of their ads.*

"I enjoy an engaging, creative campaign as much as the next guy, but what works is when brands establish and sustain meaningful, useful, and truthful relationships with their customers," writes Jonathan Baskin in *Forbes* (November 28, 2012). "Sexy, funny, engaging and all the other qualities to which we marketers aspire are really secondary, at best, and distractions, at worst." The list of campaigns we celebrate for their brilliance even though they ultimate fail is just about endless, continues Baskin, citing Dell and Gap as examples: "Gap produces iconic, visual ads as its customers wait on the sidelines until it slashes prices. Dell is held up as a model of social engagement as its sales falter."

There are two problems with the habit of evaluating advertising on its entertainment value rather than results.

First, while sales results can be measured quantitatively down to a tenth of a percent response or a dollar of revenue, entertainment is subjective; what you may think is entertaining, I may not. Therefore, evaluating advertising on its entertainment value makes the measurement of ad effectiveness purely subjective. And when the only guidance you have for an activity is based on purely subjective judgment, you are asking for trouble — because after all, what people say is just their opinion, and not fact.

The second problem with judging advertising based on its entertainment value is that the ads consumers think are the most entertaining are not the ones that educate the consumer or present product benefits. Overwhelmingly, people like ads that are funny, creative, clever, or emotional (like the horse ad discussed at the beginning of this chapter) and this is a problem because it creates the belief that if an ad is funny, creative, clever, or emotional, it must naturally be more effective than less entertaining ads.

However, there is no evidence that funny or creative ads or commercials are inherently more attention-getting and persuasive than "average" commercials.

Some advertising experts have written, most of them many years ago, that humor in advertising actually hurts response. I know of no research supporting the claim that humor either enhances or reduces the selling power of an advertisement.

So we are not saying being funny or clever in your ad is in and of itself detrimental to sales effectiveness. Certainly, there are clever and funny ads that seem to work. The AFLAC duck and the GEICO gecko are two that I suspect have done well. Stu Heinecke and others have had success using humorous cartoons in direct mail and other marketing.

However, it is not axiomatic that making your ad funny or clever automatically increases the sales it generates. And the notion that it does is what turns so many Madison Avenue ad agencies and big brand managers into circus clowns, and wastes billions of dollars on ads that don't work — because they put entertainment and creativity ahead of selling when creating ad campaigns.

"I have never agreed that creativity is the great contribution of the advertising agency," said Howard Sawyer, vice president of Marsteller, "and a look through the pages of the business magazines should dramatize my contention that much advertising suffers from overzealous creativity for self-satisfaction."

"Ads are not written to entertain," wrote Claude Hopkins in *Scientific Advertising*. "This is one of the greatest advertising faults. Ad writers forget they are salesmen and try to be performers. Instead of sales, they seek applause."

"Those of us who read the criticisms leveled at advertising around the world are constantly struck by the fact that they are not really criticisms of advertising as such, but rather of advertisements which seem to have as a prime objective finding their way into creative directors' portfolios or reels," said Keith Monk of Nestlé.

And in an article in *Advertising Age*, James Woolf writes: "The literary quality of an advertisement, per se, is no measure of its greatness; find writing is not necessarily fine selling copy. Neither is its daring departure from orthodoxy, nor its erudition, nor its imaginative conceits, nor its catchiness."

In his master's thesis at the University of Amsterdam, Graduate School of Communication, Roeland Schoppers set out to determine whether "creative" media can be more effective for health ads than traditional media. He reports:

We found no significant [difference in] results between creative media and traditional media used for recognition, attention, behavioral self-efficacy, behavioral intent, medium associated self-efficacy, or medium associated intent.

In other words, making the ads creative did not make them more effective.

Another study, this one published in the *Journal of Advertising Research* (September 2013), sought to determine whether there is an optimal level of entertainment for advertising. The research confirms that the funniest ads are not necessarily the most effective.

The study found that most advertisers believe, and research confirms, that entertainment in ads is a powerful tool to get consumers' attention and *RocketContent.com* says 84% of consumers expect brands to produce content that entertains. However, they conclude that entertainment does not necessarily make an ad effective, and further, too much entertainment could make it less impactful, as the entertainment distracts the viewer from the brand and its attributes, thereby harming comprehension.

"I have produced funny commercials in my career," says Brian, a veteran ad agency president. "Most often, people remember the joke, but not the product or service. If you have a small budget, cleverness and humor are a huge liability. An ad can be memorable and even become part of pop culture and fail to sell."

"Humor should never exist for its own sake," says Blaine, who has written direct response ratio commercials for 25 years. "I've taken comedy advertising and made it straight — and increased call volume by as much as 400% overnight."

Adds Brian: "Think of your advertising as a salesperson that you send out to bring in business. Now would you arm that salesperson with a book full of jokes? Or an urgent message that motivates someone to act?"

An article in the *Journal of Direct Marketing* confirms that "liking the advertisement is by no means a guaranteed link to sales or persuasion." An article in the Journal of Creative Disciplines cites the sock puppet for pets.com, Budweiser's Wassup, and the Taco Bell Chihuahua campaigns as three examples of creative advertising that won accolades, advertising awards, and the attention of the public but did not sell the product.

Entertainment works best when it is used to augment and communicate a sales message. Where it fails is when entertainment seems to be the ends of the commercial, the main objective, rather than a means to an ends, that ends being sales.

During the first three-quarters of 1995, Budweiser ran a campaign that scored number one in measures of noting, likeability, and memorability. During that same period, sales went down 4.3%.

Some years back, creative director Crispin Porter Bogusky was heralded as a creative genius by Madison Avenue for his edgy, imaginative commercials. One of his more famous efforts was the online campaign Subservient Chicken, where by typing commands on the keyboard, the user could control the motions of a man wearing a chicken suit.

But let's look at the results. Between 2003 — the year before Burger King hired Crispin as agency of record — and 2008, Burger King's share of the burger-chain market fell from 15.6% to 14.2%. During that same period, McDonald's share rose from 43.6% to 46.8%.

"It's not enough to have an audience watch an entertaining ad," writes Ben Parr in his book *Captivology*. "It has to generate followers, fans, and most importantly, sales."

One of the most visible and talked about "creative" campaigns was the TV commercials for the Six Flags amusement parks. The commercials featured a slightly creepy looking old geezer who danced around excitedly and implored viewers to come to the park and play.

Six Flags spend $100 million on this "creative" campaign. The result? Attendance figures declined 4% in one year. An informal survey of my colleagues in advertising found an almost 50/50 split, with half thinking the spots were funny and arresting, and the other half finding them to be stupid and obnoxious, which by the way was my view.

Another famous "creative" ad campaign that failed spectacularly was the sock puppet for Pets.com. The company spent more than $60 million on the campaign, and in those 6 months it generated only $22 million in revenues. General advertisers might defend the campaign saying it built a brand, but ROI-oriented direct marketers and business executives would consider it an enormously costly loser, returning only slightly more than a third of its cost in gross revenues.

Yet another ad campaign praised for its creativity was the

Taco Bell talking Chihuahua, which made the annual "It List" of hot trends published in *Entertainment Weekly* magazine and was also featured on the TV shows *Entertainment Tonight* and *Access Hollywood*.

During the year, Taco Bell spent an estimated $200 million in media advertising, though the company did not reveal how much of that budget went to the Chihuahua campaign.

But though the world may have found the little dog entertaining, it did not sell more tacos. Taco Bell sales fell 6% in the second quarter of 2000. The *Los Angeles Times* reported that as a result of this decline in sales, the restaurant chain put a halt to the Chihuahua campaign that people seemed to love so much.

Does this mean all creative and entertaining ad campaigns drive down sales and are failures? No, it is not axiomatic that clever ads don't work, just as it is not axiomatic that straightforward ads always work. What is axiomatic is that there is no correlations between people liking an ad and being sold by it. It certainly happens many times that ads people like also sell the product. Just not all the time. But it does some of the time.

For instance, after Ford's "Nearly Double" campaign aired during the 2014 Super Bowl, more than 50% of people who saw the TV spot rated Ford as a leader in fuel efficient vehicles, and two-thirds of people who saw the ad said it increased their opinion of the Ford brand.

DOES SEX SELL?

A related issue to entertainment in advertising is sex in advertising, which many consumers find entertaining or attention-engaging. I don't see them as quite the same thing: one is being clownish and the other merely titillating.

An article in *Advertising & Society Review* found that 20% of all magazine and web ads involve sexual images. An article in *Adweek* (6/4/12) reports that numerous studies warn that sexual imagery can be a too-risky strategy that turns off consumers, especially women, and that sex in advertising appeals to the lowest common denominator.

To define what constitutes good print advertising, we begin with what a good print ad is not:

It is not creative for the sake of being creative.

> It is not designed to please copywriters, art directors, agency presidents, or even clients.

> Its main purpose is not to entertain, win awards, or shout at the readers, "I am an ad. Don't you admire my fine writing, bold graphics, and clever concept?"

In other words, ignore most of what you would learn as a student in any basic advertising class or as a trainee in one of the big Madison Avenue consumer ad agencies.

CHARACTERISTICS OF SUCCESSFUL ADS

Okay. So that's what an ad shouldn't be. As for what an ad should be, here are some characteristics shared by successful ads:

They stress a benefit. The main selling proposition is not cleverly hidden but is made immediately clear. Example: "How to Win Friends and Influence People."

They arouse curiosity and invite readership. The key here is not to be outrageous but to address the strongest interests and concerns of your target audience. Example: "Do you Make These Mistakes in English?" appeals to the reader's desire to avoid embarrassment and write and speak properly.

They provide information. The headline "How to Stop Emission Problems — at Half the Cost of Conventional Air Pollution Control Devices" lures the reader because it promises useful information. Prospects today seek specific, usable information on highly specialized topics. Ads that provide information the reader wants get higher readership and better response.

They are knowledgeable. Successful ad copy reflects a high level of knowledge and understanding of the product and the problem it solves. An effective technique is to tell the reader something he already knows, proving that you, the advertiser, are well-versed in his industry, application, or requirement.

An opposite style, ineffectively used by many "professional" agency copywriters, is to reduce everything to the simplest common denominator and assume the reader is completely ignorant. But this can insult the reader's intelligence and destroy your credibility with him.

They have a strong free offer. Good ads contain a stronger offer. They tell the reader the next step in the buying process and encourage him to take it NOW.

All ads should have an offer, because the offer generates immediate response and business from prospects who are ready to buy now or at least thinking about buying. Without an offer, these "urgent" prospects are not encouraged to reach out to you, and you lose many potential customers.

In addition, strong offers increase readership, because people like ads that offer them something — especially if it is free and has high perceived value.

Writers of image advertising may object, "But doesn't making an offer cheapen the ad, destroy our image? After all, we want awareness, not response."

But how does offering a free ebook or white paper weaken the rest of the ad? It doesn't, of course. The entire notion that you cannot simultaneously elicit a response and communicate a message is absurd and without foundation.

Graphic techniques such as "kickers" or eyebrows (copy lines above the headline), bold headlines, liberal use of subheads, bulleted or numbered copy points, coupons, toll-free numbers set in large type, pictures of lead magnets and catalogs, dashed borders, asterisks, and marginal notes make your ads more eye-catching and response-oriented, increasing readership. On web pages, the **calls to action** (CTAs) should not be underlined phrases but large, bold, colorful buttons.

Why? My theory is that when people see a non-direct response ad or web page, they know it's just a reminder-type ad or informational web page, and figure they don't have to read it. But when they see response-type graphic devices, these visuals say to the reader, "Stop! This is a response ad! Read it so you can find out what we are offering. And respond — so you can get it NOW!"

They are clearly illustrated. Good advertising does not use abstract art or concepts that force the reader to puzzle out what is being sold. Ideally, you should be able to understand exactly what the advertiser's proposition is within five seconds of looking at the ad. As John Caples observed a long time ago, the best visual for an ad for a record club is probably a picture of CDs.

At about this point, someone branding guy from Madison Avenue will stand up and object: "Wait a minute! You said these are the characteristics of a successful direct response ad. But isn't general advertising different?"

Maybe. But one of the ways to make your general advertising more effective is to write and design it as a direct response ad. Applying all the stock-in-trade techniques of the direct marketer (coupons, toll-free numbers, free booklets, reason-why copy, benefit-headlines, informative subheads) virtually guarantees that your advertisement will be better read — and get more response — than the average "image" ad.

I agree with Howard Ruff when he says that everything a marketer does should be direct response. I think the general advertising people who claim that a free offer "ruins" their lyrical copy or stark, dramatic layout are ineffectual artists more interested in appearance and portfolios than results.

I also agree with copywriter Rich Armstrong, who states, "I've always said a person's knowledge about advertising is inversely proportional to the number of times they use the word 'brand.' "

TAKEAWAYS

Okay. What are the takeaways for this axiom?

It is axiomatic that there is no correlation between people liking an ad and being sold by it.

Some ads that people love sell a lot of product. Some ads

that people love don't sell much product if any.

Some ads that people hate or think are boring or dull sell a lot of product. Some ads that people hate or think are boring or dull don't work. There is no correlation.

Advertising professionals who view making the ad creative, clever, or beautiful are concentrating on aesthetics, which are unimportant, rather than sales, which is the objective of advertising.

Sometimes straightforward ads outperform creative ads. Other times creative ads outperform straightforward ads.

There is no rule that says creative ads don't work, as was believed by some advertising professionals in the 1800s and early 1990s. We know they can work. But being creative neither guarantees an ad's failure nor assures its success. There is simply no correlation between people liking and being entertained by an ad and the sales produced by that ad.

Thus, the widely held belief on Madison Avenue that every ad should be creative and clever is not supported by test results over many years.

So, when you sit down to create an ad, your main focus should be on "How can I sell this product?" and not "How can I create an ad everyone will admire?"

A**X**IOM™ ³
OF MARKETING

HIGH ACCURACY = HIGH RESULTS

The More Accurately You Target Your Market, the Better Your Advertising Results

In a talk presented many years ago at a New York City ad club meeting, copywriter Don Hauptman gave this valuable advice for writing copy: "Start with the prospect, not the product."

This may sound like a contradiction, but it's not.

Yes, your ad must be packed with information about the product. The information must be important to the reader: information that he will find interesting or fascinating; information that will answer his questions, satisfy his curiosity, or cause him to believe the claims you make; information, in short, that will convince him to buy your product.

CLIENT-CENTERED

The reader's own concerns, needs, desires, fears, and problems are all more important to him than your product, your company, and your goals. Good advertising copy, as Dr. Jeffery Lant points out, is "client-centered." It focuses on the prospect and how your product solves his problem. And *the more accurately your advertising targets what's important to your specific market segment, the better the results.*

For instance, instead of saying …

We have more than 50 service centers nationwide.

… translate this statement into a reader benefit …

You'll be assured of prompt, courteous service and fast delivery of replacement parts from one of our 50 service centers located nationwide.

Or, don't say …

"energy efficient"

… when you can say …

"cuts your summer electric bills in half."

The real "star" of your ad is the benefit to the particular people you are speaking to. Your product is second — and is only of concern in that it relates to a need, desire, or problem the reader has or a benefit he wants. Your company is a distant third, the least important element of your copy. It's only relevant so far as prospects want to do business with a well-known firm that has a good reputation and is financially stable.

In the 1980s, when direct mail was a dominant marketing channel, it was recognized that there were four factors that determine the response rate to a mail campaign:

> the mailing list
> the offer
> the copy
> the design

While some marketers debated which factor was the most important, the majority of experienced direct mail users agreed that the mailing list was the most critical factor in direct mail. Tests proved this to be true.[*]

Ditto copy. Occasionally, new copy could double the response rate, but usually, if the marketer could get a 25% to 50% lift in response from new copy, the copywriter was a hero.[†]

---

[*] Although there were isolated incidents of a mail package redesign doubling response, this was very rare.

[†] See the "companion" to this book, *The Axioms of Copywriting* for much more information about copywriting.

Exceptions? Of course. Offers could sometimes produce a dramatic lift in response. In one test of a mailing inviting doctors to educational seminars, adding the offer of a free pocket diary tripled response, as did the offer of a free audio CD mailed to IT professionals by a large computer company.

THE RIGHT LIST

By far the biggest lift in response usually came from testing not copy, design, or offer, but testing different lists. Our experience was the right list could pull up to ten times the response rate as the worst-performing list.

Now in direct mail, your list is your market. And we learned that the more tightly focused the list was on your ideal potential customers, the better your response rate.

The First Axiom of Marketing stated that you do not know what will work in marketing until you test it. This goes for all aspects of marketing, including, and even especially, lists.

For instance, some years ago we tested the subscriber lists of two trade journals dedicated to covering the same specific type of mid-range computer. To us, the magazines looked and read almost identical, and we could not imagine they would perform differently. But to our surprise, the subscriber list from Magazine A produced three times more inquiries from our mailing than the exact same mailing sent to the subscribers of Magazine B.

On the surface, it was seemingly inexplicable. But somehow, the publisher of Magazine A had attracted a better, more qualified readership than Magazine B — which we would never have known without testing. So if we had decided to forego testing and just rent the subscription list of Magazine B, our campaign would have been a flop instead of a success.‡

And nothing is more significant than the list or media used to reach your target audience. The closer you come to the bull's eye on the target, the more results your marketing campaign will produce.

Another big company had developed software that was specifically useful to data centers that had one mainframe computer and were going to add a second. Unfortunately, the mailing lists of the trade journals for users of that mainframe has no select indicating which subscribers were thinking of getting a second mainframe. We solved the problem by running an ad in the magazine with a headline that essentially said (this was a long time ago, so I am paraphrasing),

If you have an XYZ mainframe and are thinking of getting a second one, read this ad before you buy it.

HOW TO CHOOSE THE PERFECT LIST

Sometimes the selection of which list to mail to, or what other channel to use to reach your prospects, is obvious. At other times, it's not always apparent what list or marketing channel will reach the greatest number of your prospects and get maximum response from them at the lowest possible cost per name, per lead, or per order.

For instance, one of my clients was in the car rental business

---

‡ Yielding yet another demonstration of why in marketing you must test everything of significance.

in Florida. We wrote a letter selling coupons good for one week's car rental. You could buy a coupon book with one, four, eight, or twelve weeks' worth of coupons. In exchange, the rental fees were lower than the regular rates.

Our dilemma: What list to use. At first we thought of mailing to lists of people who vacation in Florida. But had we narrowed down our audience with enough specificity? A person who flies (not drives) to Florida typically stays for a week, so our average order would be a single coupon.

What we needed ideally was people who stayed in Florida not only for a week at a time, but for multiple weeks during the year. But who to mail to?

We tried several lists including, as I recall, Disney World visitors. But the winning list surprised us by outperforming all other lists when we tested it: a list of Florida condo owners.

Of course you can see where this makes sense. The Florida condo owners are in the state for many weeks, and if they fly down, they need to rent a car. So we got a far greater response mailing to the Florida condo owners than anyone else.

The lesson is clear: The most important thing you can do to increase your marketing results is to find and reach the right audience — the ideal buyers for your offer. The more accurately you target the right audience for what you are selling, the more sales you will make.

THE RFM FORMULA

There is a formula in direct response that is useful in identifying those prospects more likely to order from you. It is called RFM for recency, frequency, and monetary.

Recency means that those customers who have purchased most recently are the most likely to buy in response to your next promotion. If you are in fundraising, the people who have just made a donation are the ones most likely to make another donation now.

Many things in business are counterintuitive, and recency is one of them.

You would think, for example, that the person who just donated money to your charity would be the least likely to respond to another request for money right now. They just gave. Their funds are depleted. They feel they have done their bit for your cause. So they would resent being asked for even more money.

All of that sounds logical. But the truth is, those who donated the most recently are the most likely to do so again, and do it now. If you do direct mail fundraising, everyone who sends you money should get a thank-you that contains a request for even more money. Recency works!

Frequency means that customers who have ordered and bought products in your category multiple times are the most likely to order again. In direct mail, these people are called multi-buyers, and mailers pay a premium to rent the names of multi-buyers on a mailing list.

Monetary refers to how much money customers have spent on product purchases. Experience shows that you get the best results targeting prospects who have spent around the same amount of money that your product costs.

For instance, if you are promoting a $5,000 training program about real estate on the Internet via e-mail marketing, you might be tempted to rent an e-list of people who have bought a $10 book on investing in real estate because they have clearly indicated an interest in the subject of your course.

The problem is that a $10 product buyer has not demonstrated that he will buy products for $5,000 — and so the e-list of book-buyers is likely to yield minimal or no orders. Much better would be to find other promoters of expensive real estate training programs and do joint venture or affiliate deals with them.

So how do you reach those consumers who are the best prospects for what you are selling and, in doing so, increase your response and orders?

SELECTS

If you are old school and using direct mail, you will receive something called a data card which gives you detailed information about the list.

One of the things you find on data cards is "**selects**." This means you can select only those names from the list that fit specific criteria. For instance, if your product is for women, some lists let you select names by gender. If you are marketing to businesses, you can select which companies to mail based on number of employees, gross sales, geographic location, and industry.

Choosing selects slightly increases the cost per thousand names rented. But long years of experience have shown us that using selects almost always pays off — more proof that accurately identifying and marketing to the right prospects increases your marketing results.

In online marketing, one way we reach our ideal prospects is with key words, either by optimizing our web site for people searching those key words, or by choosing the right key words for our pay-per-click (PPC) advertising.

One proven method for reaching the right prospects online is to use key word phrases that identify where the prospect is in the buying process.

For instance, for someone who is thinking of buying a used car in Bergen County and has just begun to shop, the key word phrase might be "used cars Bergen County."

For prospects who are further along in the buying process, and know what make and model they want, the key word phrase might be "2018 Cadillac CTS Bergen County." That ad will connect you with the buyers you want to reach: those who want the specific model you are selling.

DEMOGRAPHICS

There are many ways to target the market so you select only those prospects who are most likely to respond to your offer. One is with demographic selection.

Demographics are tangible facts about prospects.

> Are they single or married?
> Do they have children in the house?
> Is their income over $100,000 a year?
> Is their net worth over $1 million?
> Are they high school graduates?
> College graduates?

Many postal mailing lists and to a lesser degree e-mail lists allow you to select names from the list based on these and similar criteria.

For business-to-business marketing, the demographic selections are a little different and are called *firmographics*, because they are characteristics of a firm, not an individual.

> How many employees does the company have?

> How many locations?

> What are the annual gross sales?

> What industry are they in as defined by the standard industrial classification (SIC)?

> Within the company, what is the prospect's job title and responsibilities?

> What level of education does he have?

> What kinds of products does he recommend, specify, or buy?

Consumers may also be targeted by *psychographic* characteristics defining their beliefs and behaviors.

> Are they liberal or conservative?

> Do they believe in abortion rights or gay marriage?

> Are they in fact gay themselves?[§]

The answer as to how to reach your ideal prospects is not always obvious or straightforward and often comes only with experience. For instance, if you are selling American flags, you might test a mailing list of a coin company. Why? Because coin collectors are known to be patriotic.

Likewise, if you are marketing nutritional supplements, certain lists of subscribers to conservative online newsletters have

---

§ Yes, there are gay mailing lists and media.

been known to perform well. Why? The average subscriber to political and investment newsletters is a man age 50 or older, which is the same demographic targeted by many supplement makers, especially prostate, brain, and testosterone.

Even simple targeting works, as people read and respond more if they can see themselves in the headline or subject line.

For instance, for a course on becoming an independent consultant, our subject lines focused on the six-figure income you could make being your own boss. Then we tested a subject line targeting only the older portion of our list. It read,

Read this only if you are over 50.

And the copy explained why people 50 and older have the edge in becoming independent consultants. This subject line generated double the open- and click-through rates of our control, once again showing that the more you zero-in on your ideal prospects, the more clicks, orders, and cash your marketing will generate.¶

TARGET THE "STARVING CROWD"

The most important element in reaching the right audience, one that will respond to your offer, is to make sure you are advertising a product that is potentially useful to the people reading your advertisement.

This seems to be a simple and obvious rule. Yet, many clients believe that a great ad can sell anything to anyone.

¶ In a direct mail promoting a course on how to start and run a successful consulting business, the winning headline was, *Become a consultant in your own field.*

They are wrong.

"Copy cannot create desire for a product," writes Eugene Schwartz in his book, *Breakthrough Advertising*. "It can only focus already-existing desires onto a particular product. The copywriter's task is not to create this mass desire, but to channel and direct it."

For example, no advertisement, no matter how powerfully written, will convince the vegetarian to have a steak dinner at your new restaurant. But, your ad might — if persuasively worded — entice him or her to try your salad bar.

Gary Halbert said marketers should target what he called "the starving crowd" — not people who are casual about your offer, but rather, prospects who are hungry, indeed almost desperate, for it. Those people with an urgent and immediate need. Those consumers in pain, whose worries keep them up at night and only your product can alleviate.

Charles Inlander, of the People's Medical Society, was a master at finding the right product for the right audience. Many years ago, he ran a magazine ad,

Do you recognize the seven early warning signs of high blood pressure?

That ad sold more than 20,000 copies of a book on blood pressure when it ran approximately ten times in *Prevention Magazine* over a three year period. "First, you select your topic," said Inlander, explaining the secret of his advertising success, "then you must find the right place to advertise. It's important to pinpoint a magazine whose readers are the right prospects for what you are selling."

In other words, the right product for the right audience. You will almost always be unsuccessful marketing to the wrong people — those with no interest in what you are selling — and attempting to convince them that they should be interested. As Tom Peters famously wrote in *In Search of Excellence*, "People don't argue with their own data." For instance, if you sell fine meats by mail, as Omaha Steaks does, you would be foolish to test a mailing to the subscription list of *Vegetarian Times* with an email telling them, "You really should eat meat!" The great Gene Schwartz once wrote that educating the market is too expensive and difficult. Instead, *you sell people what they already believe in.*

In every product category I have seen, the more closely you target your ideal customer, the better your sales results. An example is the niche of selling courses, systems, and software that teach how to make money by trading option contracts.

When promotions for options trading products are targeted at some of the largest and most responsive lists in investments, such as subscriber lists of investment newsletters, they often generate mediocre results. The reason is that most of these newsletters are aimed at stock and mutual fund investors. The word "options" scares them: they think it is too risky, too complicated, and too time consuming. When we take the same promotions and target them to proven "options lists" — lists of people who have already bought a course or taken a seminar on option trading — the results are significantly better. The reason is that the people on these lists have shown they are not afraid of options, and have also demonstrated that they will buy information products on options trading.

In options trading, many buyers purchase multiple systems, software, services, and courses only to be disappointed because they do not make the money promised in the advertising that sold them the product. So for an options trading software product, I wrote the headline:

Why Your Trading Software Doesn't Work . . . and Never Will.

The package pulled triple the response of the control. Clayton Makepeace calls this "entering the conversation the prospect is already having in his head." He notes that the best response comes from tapping into the prospect's dominant resident emotion — their strongest feeling about what you are selling.

Similarly, in the information technology world, IT professionals often have an adversarial relationship with the end users they serve. We wrote a headline that tapped into this dominant emotion

Important News for Any IT Professional Who Has Ever Felt Like Telling a User, 'Go to Hell.'

This generated six times the leads of the previous promotion.

Thus, the Third Axiom of Marketing is this:

The better your marketing resonates with the beliefs, desires, and feelings of your prospects, the greater the response.

Your best bet for doing that is to target those consumers who have beliefs, desires, and feelings that make them natural prospects for your product. For instance, if you sell American flags, target audiences that are patriotic, like veterans, or organizations that must fly the flag, like schools.

PLANNING YOUR MARKETING CAMPAIGN

Probably the most critical step is planning a marketing campaign to determine who you are selling to. In other words:

> Who is your audience?

> Who is the prospective buyer?

> Who will receive, read, and (hopefully) respond to your promotion?

The beauty of direct response is that you can use it to reach only those people who are potential buyers for your product or service. This is called target marketing.

For example, one management consulting firm finds that they are successful in selling their consulting programs only when they are able to reach the chief executive officer (CEO) of the client company. If they were to advertise in business magazines, they would waste a lot of money, because most of the readers are not CEOs. But they can easily rent a mailing list of CEOs and mail their message to those executives only.

"It's still important today for marketers to know their customers and to establish an ongoing means of communication with them," writes Joe Garcia in *Target Marketing* magazine. "The cornerstone of this relationship is targeting market segments — targeting peculiar, personal messages, whether by mail, phone, broadcast, or some other medium, to those who will be most receptive to the messages."

Think about your customers; are they:

> Male or female?

> Young or old?

> Rich or poor?

> New wave or old school?

> Corporate or entrepreneurial?

> City slickers or country folk?

> Married or single?

> What do they do for a living?

> Where do they live?

> What are their hobbies and interests?

If you can accurately describe your typical customer, chances are there's a list of them available.

In some cases, you may be selling one product to many different types of customers, each with different interests and concerns. In such a situation, you can use a standard brochure to describe the product in general, then tailor your **cover letter** to your different markets. For example, a financial advisor selling investments might stress low-risk in a letter to retired couples, but highlight tax-free in a letter to doctors, lawyers, and other high-income professionals.

In business-to-business (B2B) marketing, you often have to reach multiple buying influences within each client company. Let's say you're selling enterprise software to medium-size firms.

> Mail aimed at CEOs would talk about service, commitment, and your company's reputation and track record.

> A letter to the CFO could stress the cost savings and quick return on investment.

> Another letter, aimed at IT professionals, would cover the technical details and explain how the software integrates easily with existing legacy systems.

> And a fourth sales letter, sent to users, would stress the

capabilities, features, and improved productivity of the software.

The very best prospects online, however, are not those you attract with paid ads on Google, Bing, and Facebook. Nor are they people who find you via organic search. They are the people who have opted into and subscribed to your e-list.

And this is how the **Agora Model** of internet marketing works. You focus your online marketing on building your e-list. Then you sell primarily to the people on your list, not strangers.

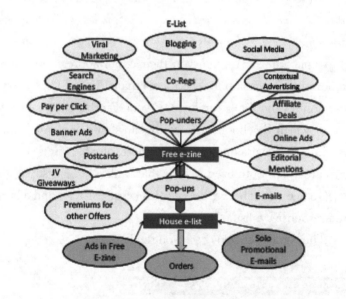

Fig. 3-1 shows the Agora Model. The ovals with arrows pointing to the rectangle labeled "free e-zine" are various meth-

ods of driving web traffic. They include

> online ads,

> e-mail marketing,

> affiliate deals,

> postcards,

> search engines,

> blog posts,

> and other traffic drivers explained throughout this book.

The goal of a traffic driver is to get the user to click on a symbol or word that is hyperlinked to a web page or form.

In the Agora model, you use the traffic drivers to send people not to your home page or a product landing page, but *to a page specifically designed for getting people to opt-in to your list by offering them a free online newsletter.* By doing so, you build your opt-in e-list of people who have given you their email address and, more important, permission to send them emails. Therefore, you own and control the list — unlike, say, your Facebook or LinkedIn group, which Facebook or LinkedIn can shut down on a whim.

In online marketing, two of the most valuable assets you can own are a well-optimized website that ranks on the first page of the Google **search engine results page** (SERP), and a large and responsive e-list.

The Agora Model is based on the latter.

THE POWER OF A NEWSLETTER

There are two reasons to send prospects an e-newsletter. The first is that to get people to opt into your e-list, you have to offer them something of value for free. An e-newsletter is such an offer. And you will get more people opting into your list if you give them an extra bonus gift as an incentive to subscribe.**

The second reason to have an online newsletter and focus on building up your subscriber list is this: When people get your newsletter, they hear from you frequently; how often depends on your publishing schedule.

As long as they remain on your list, many read at least some of the issues. Through your writing, they get to know you, feel comfortable with you, and, if you do it right, like you. And in sales, people buy from people they know and like much more readily than they do from strangers.

In addition, a number of your newsletter subscribers will email you back, making the online newsletter a two-way communication channel.

From their questions, comments, praise, and yes, even from their complaints, you will get to know this particular market — the subscribers to your e-newsletter — better than you know any other market on Earth. And, they will get to know you to. This familiarity results in both e-newsletters and email sales messages that resonate with your list, maximizing your online sales and profits.

The third axiom is rather easy to demonstrate: Write a sales email. Use your name in the "from" line. Make an offer for one of your products. Send it to (a) your e-newsletter subscribers and (b) any e-list you can rent from any list broker; choose a rental list that targets people similar to your own list.

** You can see how I do this at *www.bly.com/reports*. This is the sign-up page for my online newsletter.

HIGH ACCURACY = HIGH RESULTS

Even though the lists target a similar audience, the response from your list will invariably be much greater than the rental list. Why? You know them so well, you have targeted your message to their needs, concerns, and desires more closely than you could possibly do with an outside list.

CUSTOMER FOCUS

Always focus on the customer, and the more you can talk to him one-on-one, getting into his specific needs and concerns, the more your copy will sell. When writing copy, start with the prospect, not with the product. Your prospects are interested primarily in themselves -- their goals, their problems, their needs, their hopes, their fears, their dreams and aspirations. Your product or service is of secondary importance, the degree of concern being determined by the potential for the product or service to address one of the prospect's wants or needs, or solve one of their problems.

Effective copy speaks directly to a specific audience and identifies their preferences, quirks, behavior, attitudes, needs, or requirements. A recruitment brochure for a computer consultant firm, for example, has this headline on the cover:

Introducing a unique career opportunity only a few dozen computer professionals in the country will be able to take advantage of this year....

The headline is effective because it focuses on the prospects (IT professionals) and one of their main concerns in life (their career), rather than the consulting firm and its history, as many such brochures often do.

Write from the customer's point of view. For example,

At last you can combat the huge health insurance premiums threatening to put your small business out of business

is much better than

Introducing our Guarda-Health Employee Benefit Program.

Notice the focus on the custormer and not "our."

WEKA Publishing, in a direct mail package promoting the *Electronics Repair Manual*, a do-it-yourself guide for hobbyists and others who want to repair their own home and office electronics, uses copy that speaks directly to the personality type of the potential buyer:

If you're handy... fascinated by electronics and the world of high-tech... are happiest with a tool in your hand ... and respond to household problems and broken appliances with a defiant, "I'll do it myself"...

... then fun, excitement, the thrill of discovery, time and money saved, and the satisfaction of a job well done await you when you preview our newly updated Electronics Repair Manual at no risk for a full 30 days.

A good way to ensure that you are focusing on the prospects, and not yourself or your product or your company, is to address the prospect directly in the copy as "you." For example:

Dear Health Care Administrator:

You know how tough it is to make a decent profit margin in today's world of managed care ... and how the HMOs and other plans are putting even more of a squeeze on your margins to fill their own already-swelling coffers.

But what you may not be aware of is the techniques health care

providers nationwide are using to fight back... and get paid every
dollar they deserve for the important work they do.

This direct mail copy, which successfully launched a new publication, works because it focuses on the prospects and their problems (making money from their health care business), and not on the publication, its editors, or its features or columns.

HOW TO KNOW YOUR CUSTOMERS BETTER

Copy that fails to focus on the prospect often does so because the copywriter does not understand the prospect. If you are writing to metal shop managers, attend a metalworking trade show, read a few issues of the trade publications they subscribe to, and interview some of these prospects in person or over the phone. Study focus group transcripts, attend live focus group sessions, or even accompany salespeople on sales calls to these prospects. The better you understand your target audience, the more you have a feel for the way they think and what they think about, the more effectively you can target copy that speaks to those concerns.

In one of his lectures, AWAI co-founder Michael Masterson told his audience — mostly new and aspiring direct response copywriters — "I highly recommend you have children." Copywriter John Forde also advised his readers to have children in a recent issue of his *Copywriter's Roundtable* e-zine. Michael and John want you to have children not just to experience the joys of parenting, but because it will make you a better copywriter.

How so? The most crucial part of copywriting is your ability to understand your readers — and reach them on a deep, emotional, personal level. And the more you are like the people you are writing to … the more experiences you have shared with them … the easier it is to be empathetic with them.

I call it "experienced-based empathy." It means being able to relate to a person because you are in their group or have common experience or background.

Experienced-based empathy is a powerful technique. Not only does it enable you to get inside the minds of your prospects in a way other marketers can't. But you can actually use it in your copy to forge an instant connection with your reader, e.g., "As a CPA, I know all too well how time-consuming it is for a busy accountant like you to keep up with constant changes in the tax code."

To maximize the effectiveness of your empathy-based copy, you should target a specific market so you can hone in on their hot buttons. Of course, you cannot become a member of every target market you write for: you can't be all things to all people. A man, for example, can't be a woman (for the most part). Therefore, one can argue that a female copywriter is a better choice to write ads for feminine hygiene products, bridal gowns, or cosmetics.

As a rule, the more well-rounded your knowledge, and the more experience you have in life, the wider the range of audiences to which you can write with strong empathy and understanding. But you can't know everything about everything.

The solution? Broaden your knowledge and experiences, but do so selectively. The best areas in which to acquire new knowledge and experiences: markets you want to write for, as well as characteristics or habits that are widespread rather than unusual.

For example, if you never have children, you distance yourself from your readers who are parents. In addition, you are at a disadvantage when it comes to understanding the responsibilities and emotions of parenting, because you haven't been there.

Do I think you have to be a golfer to write good copy for golf clubs, golf balls, or golf books or videos? It's not mandatory. But if I had to choose between two copywriters of otherwise equal experience and ability to write my golf ad, and one played golf every weekend and the other had never played, I'd probably choose the golfer. If you are a golf-playing copywriter pitching a golf account, it can't hurt to let them know you're a duffer.

I do believe copywriters should pick and choose their projects based, in part, on their knowledge of and experience with the product and its market. For instance, at the beginning of my career, when I badly needed the work, a book publisher offered me a project writing direct mail packages for books on hunting and fishing. I turned down both topics — the hunting and the fishing — for slightly different reasons.

Hunting was easy: It sickens me. I love animals. I could no more write enthusiastic copy about killing a warm-blooded animal than I could write copy telling people to smoke cigarettes.

I do not have the same problem with fishing. I have gone fishing. My older son likes it, and fishes off the dock of our weekend lake house. My father loved fishing with a passion. I'll do it. But I don't love it. And so I turned down the assignment to write copy for fishing books. I understand fishing well enough to write empathetically about its positive points. Fishermen are usually nice people. But I told the client that plenty of people — including many copywriters — love to fish. I advised him to find a copywriter who is passionate about it. I only tolerate it.

In business-to-business, "becoming your prospect" can be even more difficult. I once wrote copy for a company whose products were sold to orthopedic surgeons. It was not realistic for me to become an orthopedic surgeon just to write better copy for this client.[††]

On the other hand, I knew an account executive at an industrial advertising agency assigned to a welding account. To better understand his target market, he took courses at night and became a certified welder.

I am a chemical engineer, so during the first half-decade of my career, I worked largely with industrial clients, particularly in chemical processing and related industries. Not only did I understand the client's prospects better, but engineers working for my clients felt more comfortable talking with me, knowing I was one of them and not a typical "ad guy."

When home computers were introduced, there were more copywriting opportunities in high-tech than in industrial marketing. I enrolled in night school and trained as a Certified Novell Administrator. Again, by training to become an IT professional in a class full of IT professionals, I became better able to understand and empathize with IT professionals on a deeper level.

While I'm not recommending you totally change who you are, here are some suggestions that can enable you to market

---

[††] Even if I wanted to, I couldn't get into med school.

more confidently to a broader range of prospects:

1. **Read widely** in many different fields, not just marketing.

2. **Seek out new experiences.** Snorkel, sail, rock climb, build a new deck. If you volunteer to feed the homeless at a shelter, do you think that would improve your copy to raise funds for your client's homeless shelter?

3. **See popular movies**, the ones grossing $100 million a year or more. Understand what John Q. Public likes.

4. **Get married**, have children, adopt a dog or cat (or both) from an animal shelter. This will allow you to experience emotions you might otherwise miss.

5. Whenever possible, **buy and use your clients' products**.

6. **Talk to people.** You may discover that a relative, neighbor, or friend can give you insight into a group they belong to (Vietnam veterans, boat owners, Wiccan) that you might have to sell to someday.

A✗IOM™⁴

OF MARKETING

LEAD QUALITY = 1/LEAD QUANTITY

Lead Quality is Inversely Proportional
to Lead Quantity

LEAD QUALITY = 1/LEAD QUANTITY

In lead generation marketing, the goal, as is clearly evidenced in the name, is to generate sales leads. Just so we are clear, let's define the key terms of lead-generating marketing.

An **inquiry** is a request for more information about your product or service, without regard to whether the inquirers are legitimate potential buyers or have any real interest in what you sell.

A **sales lead**, or simply "lead," is an inquiry from a qualified prospect.

A **qualified prospect** is a potential customer with the money and authority to buy what you are selling; either a strong desire to own the product, a need the product can fill, or a problem the product or service can solve; and ideally some added degree of urgency to get the need addressed or the problem taken care of.

Lead quantity is the total number of leads generated by a marketing campaign or promotion.

Lead quality is a measure of how good the lead is based on a combination of the prospect's desirability as a potential customer or client combined with how likely they are to become a customer or client of your firm (see the lead ranking section later in this chapter for a more precise discussion of quality).

Naturally, we would all love it if our campaigns generated top-quality leads by the truckload (quality *and* quantity), but this simply cannot be. Why not? Because, as this Axiom shows, it is axiomatic that things you do to generate more leads from your promotions, while indeed getting you a greater volume of potential customers, also have the undesirable side effect of boosting lead volume *at the expense of lowering lead quality.* They give you more leads, as you intended; but these leads are of a lesser quality, which is inopportune but axiomatically unavoidable.

Conversely, things you do to pre-qualify, screen, and vet prospects do in fact get you a better quality lead, but the quality improvement comes at the cost of reducing the raw number of leads.

Because the inverse correlation between lead quantity and quality is axiomatic, we cannot override it. If we use "arrows in our marketing quiver" that bump up our response rates and lead flow, it will always be at the expense of lead quality. That doesn't mean we can't get good leads. We can. It just means the methods proven to generate large numbers of leads invariably brings us many bad leads along with the good.

The good news is that, within the confines of the Axiom, it is largely within our control as to whether we go for quality or quantity in lead generation. And so, we can to a significant degree tailor the balance of volume *vs.* selectivity in our lead-flow based on the marketing tactics we select and our campaign objectives. This chapter will give you a checklist of some of the most effective marketing techniques for increasing lead volume as well as tactics known to improve the quality of your sales leads.*

QUALITY VS. QUANTITY IN SALES LEADS

The quality of sales leads can be fine-tuned like a radio. For instance, as the volume of leads goes up, the quality goes down

---

*Though, as noted, one unavoidably and always (read: *axiomatically*) inversely affects the other.

and vice versa. The slightest change in the copy and offer can produce significant changes in lead quality. So can changes in the publication, station, web page link, keywords, or e-list list used.

We refer to the relative "hardness" and "softness" of leads. A **hard lead** is super-qualified and ready to buy. Super-qualified prospects meet the MAD-FU criteria as outlined in the next section.

Soft leads are not so qualified. They are weak in at least one and most often many of the lead qualification factors of **MAD-FU**, which are:

> **m**oney to buy,

> **a**uthority to buy,

> **d**esire to buy,

> being a good **f**it for you, your business, and what you sell,

> and **u**rgency of need.

While the hard lead is the qualified prospect, on the opposite end of the spectrum in lead generation, the softest leads and inquiries are often from what are called "freebie seekers" or "collectors." These are people who just love to spend their time downloading and sending away for all the free marketing material and free content they can get. My experience is many freebie seekers never even look at what they download or send away for. The thrill or rush for them is simply getting free stuff.

THE MAD FU FORMULA

The MAD-FU (pronounced "mad eff-you") formula says that the most qualified prospects have these five common characteristics.

Money. They have a large enough budget to afford what you are selling.

Authority. They have the authority to spend that money on your product.

Desire. They very much need or want what you are selling. Either they covet the product or have an essential need or important problem your product can solve.

Fit. There is an excellent fit between what your product does and what the prospect needs it for.

Urgency. They prospect is eager to buy. They want the product soon or even immediately. They need it for a current application, not a future use.

Hard leads are often interested in talking to salespeople to get answers to questions, see a product demonstration, or get a proposal or price quotation.

A soft lead may be someone requesting free content, a free gift, a free product brochure, or other product information. They may satisfy some of the MAD-FU criteria, but not all. Soft leads never have urgency. Without urgency, the salesperson's job is much more difficult. With urgency, he is more likely to make the sale.

A prospect without urgency but with a future need is a good lead if they meet two of the other categories out of MAD-FU. For instance, if they have the money to purchase and authority to do so, you have a chance of converting them from a prospect to a buyer. If they lack money, authority, and desire, they are a poor lead and unlikely to close.

Usually we operate between the two extremes and adjust the lead flow and quality to meet immediate needs in the marketplace and to satisfy the concerns of the sales organization.

Exactly what kind of leads are needed will vary at times. Sometimes there will be too many that don't pan out into sales. Other times there won't be enough leads to keep the sales staff busy.

HOW TO IMPROVE LEAD QUALITY

If dealers or salespeople complain about the quality of leads, here's how to bring in leads that have been "hardened" through changes in advertisements or digital marketing:

Mention price. Indicate what the product will cost.

Mention sales call. Say someone will call.

Make any information offered directly relevant to the product or the application only. The logic is that a person will not send for a white paper on managing UNIX data centers unless he manages a UNIX data center.

Tell more. Reveal more information about the product, including any potential negatives.

Ask for more information from the prospect. Get the telephone number, email address, company name, location, person's job title, and the best hours to call. If conducting business direct marketing, ask how many employees the company has, as well as other information that might be useful.

Ask the prospect if they just want the free "bribe" of a white paper or report you are offering, or would also like information about the product or service you are selling, and also if they are interested in getting a proposal, cost estimate, or otherwise speaking more about potential purchase of the product or service; see the sample "Lead Qualification Landing Page

(**LQLP**)" (see page 73). The LQLP helps qualify leads because those responders who request an estimate, sales call, or more information on the specific products or services you sell are somewhat more qualified than those who just say "send me the free lead magnet only."

On web pages for downloading free content offers or otherwise making inquiries, asking a lot of questions requires having many fields of information for the prospect to fill in, and making these fields mandatory, meaning if the prospect does not fill in a required field, he cannot submit his request and get his free white paper or ebook.

Charge something. Even a token amount for a special report, ebook, or sample will smoke out real deadbeats. A common content offer is to give away a physical book or DVD free, but charge a nominal amount for shipping and handling.

For direct mail, require prospects to provide their own stamp. Don't use a business reply card or envelope. Let the prospects buy the stamps and maybe even supply their own envelopes.

Narrow the offer. Make it very relevant to the product or service you are selling.

Don't offer a free gift to people making inquiries, such as the pens or calculators offered by some reverse mortgage and insurance companies advertising on TV or in the AARP member's magazine.

Do not offer free content such as a book, white paper, or special report. Only offer product literature such as a brochure or catalog.

LEAD QUALITY = 1/LEAD QUANTITY

HOW TO INCREASE LEAD QUANTITY

On the other hand, if you need lots more leads rather than just great quality leads, here's how you can loosen up the lead quality and obtain many more inquiries from the same promotion expenditures:

Tell less. Leave something to curiosity.

Pre-populate landing pages, which you can do with a personalized URL (pURL); when the prospect clicks on the pURL or enters it into her browser, the page that appears is already filled out with her information. All she has to do is click submit. For direct mail, fill in the names and addresses of the prospects on the reply card. Give the prospects less to do.

Add convenience. Supply the stamp, the envelope, and maybe even a pencil in a direct mail promotion. Online, give a discount.

On a landing page, ask almost no questions. If you ask questions, make answering as many as you can optional, not required fields.

For telephone response, ask no qualifying questions. If you have promised to send an information kit, just get the prospect's contact information. Don't ask when they are thinking of making a purchase or how interested they really are.

Give more. Add a free gift or premium, maybe one that has value independent of the product offered. For instance, one direct mail package for agriculture chemicals sent to farmers offered a free football for the farmer's kids to play with in return for the name and phone number of a neighbor farmer who might also be interested in the fertilizer.

New Free e-Book Reveals 35+ Years of Tested B2B Marketing Secrets

Since 1979, freelance copywriter Bob Bly has written hundreds of winning B2B promotions – including landing pages, white papers, e-mail marketing campaigns, ads, and sales letters – for over 100 clients including IBM, AT&T, Praxair, Associated Global Systems, Intuit, Ingersoll-Rand, and Medical Economics.

Now, in Bob's 186-page e-book *The Business-to-Business Marketing Handbook*, you'll discover 30+ years of tested B2B marketing secrets, including:

Yours FREE – Bob Bly's B2B Marketing Handbook!

- 10 tips for increasing landing page conversion rates – page 10.
- The 6 key components of effective B2B offers – page 19.
- What's working in e-mail marketing today?—page 112.
- 7 tips for more effective content marketing—page 78.
- Best practices for B2B lead generation—page 54.
- 4 steps to writing SEO copy that both your prospects and the search engines will love—page 49.
- 5 ways to build a large and responsive e-list of prospects--page 29.
- How to write technically accurate copy for high-tech products -- page 143.
- And more....

Bob Bly | Copywriter/Consultant | 31 Cheyenne Dr., Montville, NJ 07045 |
Phone: 973-263-0562 | www.bly.com | E-mail: rwbly@bly.com

To see whether you qualify for a FREE copy of The Business-to-Business Marketing Handbook, just fill in the form below and click submit now:

*Required field

* Please send me:

☐ FREE copy of The Business-to-Business Marketing Handbook.
☐ FREE Copywriting Information Kit with details on Bob's copywriting services including a fee schedule.
☐ FREE no-obligation estimate for a copywriting project.

* Name:

* Title:

* Company:

* Website URL:

* E-mail Address:

* Phone

* Verify   CBE8B

Submit!

Offer valuable free content such as lead magnets.

Offer content and items not related to your product. For instance, a free calendar or pen and pencil set or flashlight.

Use free offers. Make it free, free, free. And say it is **free**. Be explicit. Say "FREE" and shout it out in big, bold, large, all-caps. Don't say "complimentary." If a thing is free, say it is free. No cost. Not one thin dime. On us. You get the idea.

Add a prize. A sweepstakes is the ultimate quality-softener.

And remember that the choice of media will also have a material effect on lead quality. The low-cost-per-lead publication or list may be composed of teenagers, retirees, or other brochure collectors who send for everything. Study the source data and change mailing list and media selection to improve quality. Fine-tuning the media is just as important as fine-tuning the offer.

LEAD-RANKING

Once you evaluate the quality of a lead with the MAD-FU system, you can then rank all leads generated by the campaign according to quality.

You can use whatever lead-ranking system you wish. One of the most popular is called "**probability ranking**."

With probability ranking, you assign each lead a number representing your best guess as to how likely the lead is to close and become a customer. A 0.9 means you estimate the probability of this prospect becoming a customer is approximately 90 percent; a 0.5 means it is 50-50.

You then list all leads in order of highest to lowest probability, and concentrate your follow-up sales efforts on those leads nearest the top of the list, which will have probability ratings of 70 percent or higher.

Leads can also be ranked using the "metal" system, which indicates the desirability of any lead becoming a customer or client according to four levels of ranking: copper, silver, gold, and diamond, as follows:

Copper. These prospects are the least desirable potential new clients. They do not have a lot of money. They are not a great fit for your business for any number of reasons; *e.g.*, they are too far out of town; they are in a niche you don't serve; on the phone they seem difficult or unpleasant to deal with, *etc*. You only pursue copper leads when you are really desperate and need the business. Otherwise, you just send them the brochure or white paper they asked for, add them to your e-mail prospect list, and don't follow up beyond that. They are not worth the time, effort, and aggravation.

Silver. Somewhat better than copper. They are far from ideal clients, but some are acceptable enough, and others a bit better than that. Most businesses are happy to follow up silver leads and convert them. Many have the potential to become good clients that help you pay the bills.

Gold. Gold prospects are those whom you would love to have as customers or clients. They are easy to work with, appreciate what you provide, and expect to pay a reasonable sum for good value received. Gold prospects are or at least should be the primary target for your lead-generating marketing campaigns. These are the prospects you want to do business with, and they are worth pursuing until you get them.

Diamond. When you target gold, or even if not, you occasionally get leads from diamond prospects. These are the "dream" clients, the customers you and your competitors all rightly covet. They will pay top dollar for great products and services delivered reliably and on time. And if they like you, they will favor you with a ton of repeat business.

Another common lead-ranking system is called "**opportunity ranking**." You rate each lead on a scale of 1 to 10 based on its potential profit value. The leads representing the best opportunity to close a profitable new account are ranked 10 and those that are junk are ranked 1. The number assigned takes into consideration several factors including:

> How likely the lead is to close.

> Whether the prospect is copper, silver, gold, or diamond.

> The potential for this account to generate lucrative repeat orders.

> The potential for a long-term vs. a short-term or one-shot business relationship with this customer.

> The estimated lifetime customer value (**LTCV**).

Lifetime customer value is the amount of money this customer will spend with your company for the duration of their business relationship with you. For instance, if the customer subscribes to your cable TV service for $89/month, and stays with your cable system for 3 years before canceling service or switching to satellite dish, the LTCV is

$89/month x 12 months x 3 years = $3,204

Knowing your LTCV gives you a huge advantage in marketing over any competitors that do not know their LTCVs. Going back to our cable TV example, a competitor who does not understand LTCV often sets their "marketing spend" — the amount of money they are willing to spend on advertising to acquire a new customer — at or below the value of the first order or initial payment.

So if the cable service is $89 a month, they are reluctant to spend more than that to acquire a new customer, and the lack of funds limits their marketing reach and effectiveness. Even if they were smart enough to realize the first month's sale is just that, the first of many months of payments, and set the marketing budget for customer acquisition at the price of a full month of cable service, they'd only have $89 to spend.

On the other hand, the cable provider who has a $3,204 LTCV and knows they have it will realize they can send many multiples of $89 to acquire a new customer and still be wildly profitable. A marketing budget for new customer acquisition set at just 10% of the $3,204 LTCV would be $320 per new account, enabling them to outspend their $89 competitor more than 3 to 1.

THE MOTIVATING SEQUENCE

In the copywriting of marketing materials, there is a proven 5-step sequence called **The Motivating Sequence** that most persuasive promotions follow. The five steps of the motivating sequence are as follows:

Step 1: Get attention. Before your promotion can do anything else, it has to get your prospect's attention. It must get the prospect to stop, open the envelope, and start reading the materials inside instead of tossing your mailing in the trash.

You already know many methods of getting attention, and see dozens of examples of them in action every day. In TV and magazine advertising, sex is often used to gain attention for products ranging from soft drinks and cars to diets and exercise programs.

Or, you can,

> make a bold statement,

> cite a startling statistic,

> ask a curiosity-arousing question,

> put a bulky object in the envelope,

> or use a pop-up graphic.

You get the idea.

Step 2: Identify the problem or need. Most products fill a need or solve a problem that a group of prospects are facing. But what are the chances that the prospect is thinking about this problem when she gets your promotion? Probably not great.

So the first thing you have to do is to focus the prospect's attention on the need or problem your product addresses. Only then can you talk to them about a solution.

For instance, if you are selling an economical office telephone system, instead of starting off by talking about your system, you might say,

Are you sick and tired of skyrocketing long-distance phone bills?

Step 3: Position your product as the solution to the problem. Once you get the prospect to focus on the problem, the next step is to position your product or service as the solution to that problem. This can be a quick transition. Here's an example from a fundraising letter from the Red Cross:

Dear Mr. Bly:
Some day, you may need the Red Cross.
But right now, the Red Cross needs you.

Step 4: Proof. As Mark Joyner points out in his book *The Irresistible Offer* (John Wiley & Sons, 2005), one of the questions at the tip of your prospect's tongue upon receiving your promotion is, "Why should I believe you?"

You answer that question by offering proof. That proof is of two sorts.

The first type of proof goes to credibility. It convinces the prospect that you, the seller, are a reputable firm or individual, and therefore someone to be trusted. A diploma from a prestigious medical school displayed prominently on a doctor's office wall is an example of proof of credibility.

The second type of proof has to do with the product, and convinces the buyer that your product can do what you say it can do. Testimonials, case histories, reviews, performance graphs, and test results are examples of proof in this category.

Step 5: Action. The final step is to ask for action. Your goal is usually to generate either an inquiry or an order.

To ask for action in direct marketing, we make an "offer." I define the offer as

> *what the reader gets when she responds to your promotion, combined with what she has to do to get it.*

In a lead-generating direct mail package, the offer might be as simple as "mail back the enclosed reply card for our free catalog."

In an online promotion, the offer might be "click here, enter your credit card information, and purchase our product on a 30-day money back trial basis for $49.95 plus $4.95 shipping and handling."

I am willing to wager that every successful piece of copy you have ever mailed or e-mailed follows, to some extent, the steps in the motivating sequence — even if you've never heard of it before. That's because you have an instinct for how to sell, and that instinct leads you to organize your selling arguments according to the motivating sequence.

So, if you can sell instinctively, then what use is knowing **AIDA**, the motivating sequence, or other persuasion formulas?

The answer is this: when you have the steps written out in front of you, you can more consciously make sure that you've handled all five steps fully and in correct sequence — and make sure no step is short-changed or left out — increasing your odds of writing a winner.

GENERATE MORE LEADS FROM PRINT ADS

Here are 29 techniques for generating more leads from print ads.

1. Ask for action. Tell the reader to phone, write, contact his sales rep, request technical literature or place an order.

2. Offer free information, such as a color brochure or catalog.

3. Describe your brochure or catalog. Tell about its special features, such as a selection chart, planning guide, installation tips or other useful information it contains.

4. Show a picture of your brochure or catalog.

5. Give your literature a title that implies value. "Product Guide" is better than "catalog." "Planning Kit" is better than "sales brochure."

6. Include your address in the last paragraph of copy and beneath your logo in type that is easy to read. (Also place it inside the coupon, if you use one).

7. Include a toll free number in your ad.

8. Include your website's URL.

9. Put a small sketch of a telephone next to the phone number. Also use the phrase, "Call toll-free."

10. Create a hot line. For example, a filter manufacturer might have a toll-free hot line with the numbers 1-800-FIL-TERS. Customers can call the hot line to place an order to get more information on the manufacturer's products.

11. For a full-page ad, test using a coupon. It will increase response 25% to 100%.

12. Make the coupon large enough that readers have plenty of room to write in their name and address.

13. Give the coupon a headline that affirms positive action, such as "Yes, I'd like to cut my energy costs by 50% or more."

14. Give the reader multiple response options. Such as,

> *I would like to . . .*
> *. . . see a demonstration*
> *. . . have a salesperson call*
> *. . . receive a free planning kit by return mail.*

15. For a fractional ad-one-half page or less-put a heavy dashed border around the ad. This creates the feel and appearance of a coupon, which in turn stimulates response.

16. In the closing copy for your fractional ad clearly state your free offer.

17. A bound-in-business reply card, appearing opposite your ad, can increase response by a factor or two or more.

18. Use a direct headline, one that promises a benefit or stresses the offer of free information rather than a headline that is cute or clever.

19. Put your offer of a free booklet, report, selection guide or other lead magnet in the headline of your ad.

20. Offer a free gift, such a slide rule, metric conversion fable, pocket ruler, *etc.*

21. Offer a free product sample.

22. Offer a free consultation, analysis, recommendation, study, cost estimate, computer printout, etc.

23. Talk about the value and benefits of your free offer. The more you stress the offer, the better your response.

24. Highlight the free offer in a copy subhead. The last subhead of your ad could read, "Get the facts . . . Free."

25. In a two-page ad, run copy describing your offer in a separate sidebar.

26. Be sure the magazine includes a reader service number in your ad.

27. Use copy and graphics that specifically point the reader to your phone number or URL.

28. Test different ads. Keep track of how many inquiries each ad pulls. Then run only those ads that pull the best.

29. Look for a sales appeal, key benefit, or theme that may be common to all of your best-pulling ads. Highlight that theme in subsequent ads.

MORE LEADS FROM DIRECT MAIL

Here are 50 lead-generating tips for **direct mail**.

1. How many steps are there in the buying process for this

product? Where in this process does my mailing fit?

2. What can I tell my prospect that will get him to take the next step in the buying process?

3. Can I reduce selling costs by creating a mailing designed to produce a direct sale instead of an inquiry?

4. How many leads do I want to generate? Do we want a large quantity of "soft" leads? Or are we better off getting a smaller number of more highly qualified leads?

5. What happens if the mailing produces too many leads? Too few?

6. Is there a geographic region that my sales force does not cover? How can I respond to inquiries from this region?

7. What is the primary market for my product or service? (Which industry needs it most?)

8. Are there any secondary markets for the product large enough to justify a custom-tailored version of the mailing?

9. Who is my primary prospect within the target industry? What is his or her job title? Function?

10. Who are the other people (by job title) involved in the purchase decision for this product? What are their roles? (Who recommends the product? Who specifies it? Who has authority to approve the purchase?)

11. Must we reach all of these prospects? Or can we generate the desired sales result by targeting only one or two key decision makers at each prospect organization?

12. If we don't know who we should be mailing to, how can we find out? From our sales representatives? Market research? Direct mail?

13. If we don't know what we should be telling our potential customers about our product, how can we find out?

14. Should we tailor versions of our sales letter either to vertical markets or various job titles - or both?

15. Should we tailor our brochure to specific markets or job titles?

16. What offer are we using in our current mailing? Is there a way to make the offer stronger or better?

17. Is the prospect in need of information about our product or the problem it solves? Can we package this information in a booklet or report and offer it as a lead magnet in our mailing?

18. Does our sales process involve a face-to-face meeting with the prospect? Can we legitimately call this sales meeting a "free consultation" and feature it as the offer in our mailing?

19. Do we allow the user to sample our product on a free trial basis? Should we be stressing this free trial offer in our mailing?

20. Do we offer our mail customers a free gift, price discount, free shipping and handling, or other money-saving incentive for responding to our mailing? If not, why not?

21. What reason or incentive can we give the reader to respond NOW and not later?

22. Can we use telemarketing to qualify sales leads generated by our direct mail program?

23. Can we use telemarketing to turn non-responders into responders?

24. Can we use telemarketing to identify and pre-sell prospects before we send them our mailing package?

25. What format is best for our mailing? Full-blown direct mail package (letter, brochure, reply card)? Or sales letter only?

26. Is there any benefit to personalizing the mailing?

27. What graphic treatment is appropriate for our audience? Should it be businesslike or bright and loud? Should it be "disguised" as personal correspondence or clearly marked (by use of teaser and graphics) as direct mail?

28. What copy approach should I use? Serious or breezy? Educational and informative vs. hard sell?

29. Does my reader want or need a lot of information?

30. Can I use a self-mailer format?

31. Is a post card appropriate for my offer?

32. Should I use a single mailing or a series of mailings?

33. How many mailings should I send to my list before giving up on people who do not respond?

34. In a series of mailings, am I using a variety of different sizes and formats to gain attention for my message?

35. Are request for more information fulfilled within 48 hours?

36. Are hot sales leads separated for immediate follow up by sales representatives or telephone salespeople?

37. What is the conversion ratio (the percentage of inquiries that result in a sale)?

38. Are our salespeople competent? If not, what can we do to ensure better handling of sales leads?

39. Do salespeople follow up on all leads provided? If not, why not?

40. Do salespeople welcome direct mail leads or do they grumble about them? Why?

41. Are there qualifying questions we can add to our reply form to help salespeople separate genuine prospects from "brochure collectors"?

42. Can we afford to send a hard copy catalog or CD to everyone who requests it?

43. Do we have a sufficient quantity of sales literature on hand to fulfill all requests for more information (assuming we get a 10% response to our mailing)?

44. Do we get a better quality lead by requiring the prospect to put a stamp on the reply card rather than offering a postage-paid business reply card?

45. Do we get better sales results from prospects who respond by telephone or online versus those who mail in reply cards?

46. Does our fulfillment package or sales brochure provide the prospect with the information he asked for? And does it do a good job of selling our product or service?

47. Do we include a cover letter with the brochures and product data sheets we send in response to mail-generated inquiries?

48. Do we include a questionnaire, spec sheet, or some other type of reply form with our inquiry fulfillment package?

49. Do we automatically send follow-up mailings and emails to prospects who don't respond to the inquiry fulfillment package?

50. Should we be more vigorous in our program of follow-up mailings, phone calls, and emails?

MORE LEADS WITH CONTENT MARKETING

Content marketing means generating sales leads by offering potential customers free information. Examples of popular free content offers in marketing campaigns include

> > white papers,
> > special reports,
> > ebooks,
> > eclasses,
> > and webinars.

We call these pieces of free content **lead magnets**, because they are intended to attract more leads, much like a real magnet attracts iron filings.

Do lead magnets work? Both in theory and in practice, yes, content marketing works. On average, a marketing campaign for a product or service that offers a good lead magnet will attract twice as many sales leads as the same campaign without the free lead magnet offer.

However, there is a dark side. Even though offering a free lead magnet doubles the number of leads generated, a lot of those leads are usually of inferior quality. What happens is this: Yes, you get more leads. But many of those inquiries come, unfortunately, from people who are not as much interested in buying your product or service as they are getting something free.

If you are as interested in building your opt-in e-list as generating lead, this may be okay for you. However, if you are much more concerned about getting new business, and not getting opt-ins or giving away free content, the weaker quality of leads from content marketing campaigns can be problematic.

LEAD QUALITY = 1/LEAD QUANTITY

The problem of getting "bad leads" from free content offers is exacerbated when you factor in the time wasted and the
frustration experienced by your sales force. Salespeople hate it
when they are given leads from marketing that in fact do not
turn out to be leads at all, but merely requests for a freebie. It
gets even worse: When a lot of the leads produced by content
marketing campaigns are of questionable quality, the sales team
begins questioning the value of all of these leads. Result: The
truly good leads may be given short shrift or bypassed altogether,
losing sales.

The good news, though, is that content marketing has what
I call a **net positive lead return on investmen**t (NPLROI).
NPLROI means that, even when you throw away the bad leads
produced by a strong content offer, the good news is that there
are still more good leads produced than there are than what the
same promotion yields without the free lead magnet offer. So
on a net positive ROI basis, content marketing generates more
good leads, prospects, and clients than marketing without a free
content offer.

Content marketing is inherently strong for two reasons:
First, educated consumers are your best customers, and the content educates the consumer about the product, its usage, and
the purchase decision. And second, it boosts overall response
rates, because free is one of the two most powerful words in the
copywriter's toolkit.[†]

But it has an inherent flaw because of this Axiom of Marketing which states that lead quality is inversely proportional to lead

---

[†] The other one is "you."

quantity. By offering the content bribe, we get more leads, but their quality suffers and so we get numerous inquiries from unqualified prospects, which waste our time and have a poor closing rate.

Fortunately, with the simple techniques in this chapter, you can fine-tune your lead-generation campaigns to achieve the desired balance between lead quantity and lead quality.

And to generate not just inquiries and requests for free downloads, but instead actually get qualified leads from your on-line marketing, use the lead qualification landing page as shown on page 73.

on page 73.

BOTTOM LINE

Despite the drawback of producing a large number of unqualified leads, content marketing with lead magnet offers is still the best practice for lead generation marketing today. In the 21st century, I always have some sort of free content offer the lead generation campaigns I create — and you always should, too.

AXIOM™ 5

OF MARKETING

KNOWLEDGE IS FINITE

It Is Impossible to Know or Master
Every Tactic, Old and New, in the Field
of Marketing

KNOWLEDGE IS FINITE

Today people in almost every profession and walk of life are suffering from information overload: there is too much to know and too much new information being created every day that keeping up is impossible.

This is a phenomenon of the modern age and it is here to stay. Never again will a person in any field in general, and marketing in particular, be able to keep up with all the new developments and knowledge ever again. Decades ago, Thomas Edison recognized this when he famously said, "We don't know one-millionth of one percent about anything."

Until 1900, human knowledge doubled approximately every century. By the end of World War II, knowledge was doubling every 25 years.

In the 21st century, human knowledge is doubling every eighteen months. IBM claims that the build-out of the "Internet of things" will one day lead to the doubling of knowledge every twelve hours. *Forbes* reports that by at least one calculation, we have created more information in the last ten years than in all of human history before that.

According to the web site *infoengineering.net,*

information overload is when you are trying to deal with more information than you are table to process to make sensible decisions. It is now commonplace to be getting too many e-mails, reports, and incoming messages to deal with them effectively.

As a result, so many businesspeople today are suffering from "marketing information overload." By that, I mean they are bombarded constantly with marketing information, facts, statistics, and advice. An article in *The Economist* notes that this information overload, and the anxiety people experience attempting to keep up with it, is called by a variety of labels including "data asphyxiation" and "information fatigue."

For instance, I must at this point receive over a dozen marketing e-newsletters Not to mention the endless invitations to both webinars and live seminars, conferences, and boot camps.

An online newsletter I received today had as its lead article, "3 Tips for a Successful Snapchat Presence." I have never been on Snapchat in my life, have no Snapchat presence, and do not intend to. Social media drowns us in trivial content.

The offers for more marketing books, e-books, courses, podcasts, and training programs never stop. Plus, already successful entrepreneurs and marketing managers are continually getting the hard-sell from copywriters, consultants, SEO vendors, ad agencies, and other marketing services firms saying "buy my program" or "hire me."

This puts many marketers in a situation where they don't quite know what to do.

They are afraid that if they don't read, watch, and listen to everything and everyone, they will miss an idea that could be beneficial to their business.

And they are right — they will.

On the other hand, you can't read, watch, and listen to all of the marketing content pushed out to you each day — or really, even more than a tiny fraction of it.

If you tried, it would consume your entire work day — more than that, every waking hour — and even then you still wouldn't make much of a dent in it.

OVERCOMING OVERLOAD

Fortunately, I have three solutions to rescue you from this marketing information overload.

First up is my **25-50-25 rule of time management** at work. It says that no more than 25% of your time should be spent on educating yourself in marketing and other business topics.

As for the rest of your time, 50% or more should be on doing your core business function, and no more than 25% on "administrivia" — everything from filling out time sheets, to organizing your files, to having staff meetings, to organizing the company picnic, to social media posting, to marketing your services, to talking with prospects.

The second solution to combating marketing information overload is to understand what I call "**The Iceberg Theory of Marketing**." This theory says that you can be wildly successful in business using only a small percentage of the many dozens of marketing channels and methods available to you — and ignoring the rest.

The third solution is to cut way back on collecting and buying content. For instance, if you bought a course on Internet information marketing, go through that course and start applying the lessons before you buy and take another course.

Too many marketers are frozen by "analysis paralysis." They spend too much time studying and thinking about marketing, and not enough time actually doing marketing. Remember: Ideas without action yield zero results.

Related to information flow is the problem of "Big Data." Big data as the trade press uses the term means a collection of data too large for traditional database management systems, analytics packages, and other tools to handle. In 2012, Gartner defined big data as follows:

> *Big data is high volume, high velocity, and/or high variety information assets that require new forms of processing to enable enhanced decision making, insight discovery, and process optimization.*

We need computers to make sense of big data; the human mind simply cannot process big data or even much data at all. Research studies show that the human working memory can only temporarily store three to seven items — no more. By temporary storage, we mean the items are at the forefront of our mind, available for instant recall and processing.

The long-term storage capacity of the human brain is much larger. The human brain has about one billion neurons, each forming 1,000 connections to other neurons, for a total of more than a trillion connections. This results in the brain having a total memory storage capacity of about a million gigabytes, which is 2.5 petabytes.

But in practice, data doesn't have to be petabytes or even terabytes to be "big." Any amount of data that a marketer can't easily analyze and convert into meaningful, actionable insights can be considered "big data," at least as far as the owner of the data is concerned.

T-Mobile, for instance, pooled data through their IT structures for customer transactions and interactions. By leveraging this data with Customer Relationship Management (CRM) and billing system transaction data, T-Mobile reportedly cut customer defections in half in a single quarter.

Trident Marketing, a direct response and sales firm, constructed a data warehouse to collect thousands of data points from internal databases and external sources. An analytics solution was then used to determine which customers were most likely to buy which products, and when. The company increased sales tenfold over four years while reducing marketing costs 30%.

For direct response and digital marketers, the critical skill is to translate what your data tells you into actionable marketing ideas that improve results, regardless of how much data are involved.

A McKinsey analysis of more than 250 engagements over five years revealed that companies who put data at the center of their marketing and sales decisions improve their marketing return on investment (ROI) by up to 20 percent. That adds up to $15 to 27 billion of additional value based on global annual digital ad spend of an estimated $136 billion.

But what if you, like a lot of marketers, are drowning in a sea of data you can't seem to navigate or put to work making you money?

The solution to making sense of your data, regardless of size, is to create an infrastructure capable of taking whatever amount of data you typically collect and using it to guide you in making profitable marketing decisions.

As I'll discuss in a minute, you have two choices: building this infrastructure in-house or retaining the services of data companies that already have these infrastructures in place.

For instance, a specialty wholesale manufacturer of lighting fixtures was seeing a decline in catalog response rates and revenues. The catalog company's house file had recency, frequency, and monetary (RFM) on all records. The company hired a data services vendor to append SIC codes, location type, sales volume, employee size, and other firmographic data to the records. By profiling and analyzing the data against prior mail files, the data vendor identified specific attributes which pointed to greater performance. Using those attributes, the data services firm built a custom model and applied it to the cataloger's prospecting database. Multivariate models can forecast items such as response rates, average sales, customer lifetime value, ROI, and customer attrition. Model scores are developed using regression analysis. The model identified records that weren't performing, so the marketer could eliminate mailings to the least responsive names.

The result was a 46% increase in response rates in the aggregate across all segments. Modeled names outperformed non-modeled names by 1.5 to 1. ROI increased 91%.

But as with other forms of information load, even large organizations cannot keep up with big data. The Economist Intelligence Unit found 35% of executives lack an understanding of how to apply big data, and 62% of CIOs report big data buzz has resulted in unrealistic expectations among executives.

But whether it's big data or too many webinar invitations, we are bombarded by marketing information. We can never keep up. And for the reasons noted in this chapter, we shouldn't even try: Information overload is here to stay, and we have to combat it to survive and stay productive and profitable.

But for marketers, there is a silver lining to the cloud of data and information: namely, you don't have to know everything about marketing, or even most things about marketing, to be tremendously successful at it.

The fact is, despite there being dozens of marketing channels available to us today, the top marketers use primarily only a handful: the few they know best, are most comfortable with, and have had the most success in.

Ben Settle, for example, focuses almost exclusively on email marketing, while the late Clayton Makepeace specialized in sales letters, and Bob Reina of Talk Fusion is heavily weighted toward video marketing. Facebook founder Mark Zuckerberg became fabulously wealthy with only social media, while Larry Page, cofounder of Google, did that same thing with search. Perry Marshall built his Internet marketing empire on mastery of Google advertising. Mark Bruce specialized in public relations for high-tech companies.

Others simplify their lives by honing in on marketing in one specific and often narrow niche. I know a guy with a small ad agency that does nothing but marketing for audiologists and hearing aids. Another consultant, a guy I went to high school with, does marketing and business management strictly for eye doctors.

So take the *Fifth Axiom of Marketing* to heart and realize that you'll never know everything about marketing — and that's okay. Because you only have to find that one technique or niche and master it and you can make your fortune.

Now ask yourself, what's yours?

A**X**IOM™ ⁶
OF MARKETING

EMOTION > FACTS

In All Marketing, Emotion is Stronger
Than Features, Benefits, and Facts

EMOTION > FACTS

It is widely accepted among successful marketers and sales-people that emotion is stronger than logic when it comes to selling to the general public. Several studies conclude that up to ninety percent of the decisions we make are based on emotion; we use logic only to justify our choices and actions to ourselves and to others.

An article in *The Atlantic* observes,

> *The most successful ads have broad emotional and cognitive appeal. They target aspiration, persuasion, and emotion — what Clay Warren, director of the Communications Program at George Washington University, labels ethos, logos, and pathos.*

In his book *Descartes Error*, neuroscience professor Antonio Damadio says that emotion is a necessary ingredient in almost all decision.

One piece of evidence supporting the importance of emotion in decision-making comes from a study published in the journal *Brain and Cognition*. It found that people with damage to a part of the brain that processes emotion, and who as a result are no longer able to process emotional information, have impaired decision-making capabilities which seriously compromise the quality of decisions in daily life.

According to *Psychology Today*, advertising research reveals that emotional response to an ad has far greater influence on a consumer's reported intention to buy a product than the ad's content by a factor of 3-to-1 for TV commercials and 2-to-1 for print ads. MRI neuro-imaging shows that when evaluating brands, consumers primarily use emotions, personal feelings, and experiences rather than product features and facts.

Negotiation expert Jim Camp writes,

Decision-making isn't logical, it's emotional. In fact, even with what we believe are logical decisions, the very point of choice is arguably always based on emotion.

Sales expert Gerhard Gschwandter said that "selling is a transfer of emotion that comes from two sources: logic and emotion."

The late Zig Ziglar said that logic accounted for only 20% of the persuasion in selling, with appeals to emotion being the remaining 80%.

MARKETING TO B2B

But the superiority of emotion over logic in persuasion leading to purchase decisions is not universally accepted among B2B marketers, where there are two schools of thought concerning marketing to business and technical buyers.

The first school says, "Copy should be as short as possible, direct, and to the point. Bullet lists are better than sentences and paragraphs. Don't do any selling. Just give business buyers the facts, data, and specifications they need to make an intelligent decision about buying your product. No need to state the benefits. They already know they need the product and why. You just have to convince them that your brand is superior to other products in the category you compete against, and that your product satisfies their application's requirements."

Advocates of this "rational" school of B2B marketing believe that business prospects, at work, are largely rational beings who make logical decisions based on facts. They strive to keep written communications as short as possible, in the belief that all businesspeople are extremely busy with no time to read.

"Business-to-business copy should be completely fact-based," says LT, a veteran B2B marketer. "And the less there is to read in your copy, the greater your response rates will be. Long copy in B2B gets tossed in the trash." LT also advises that copy written for B2B audiences should sound professional rather than conversational. "These are educated people," he says, "and you must talk to them on their own level, which is high."

The other school of B2B marketing is the "emotional" school. Their philosophy was articulated to me by HF, who owned a successful industrial ad agency in the 1980s. HF said: "The business prospect doesn't stop being a person when he sets foot in the office. He is a human being first, and an executive or engineer second. Therefore, the same psychological factors motivate him as a human being whether he is at work or at home."

The emotional school of B2B marketing uses copy and design that reads and looks more like consumer advertising than technical writing. The copy style is personal and conversational, tapping into the prospect's needs, concerns, fears, and desires.

"Because business customers are persons, communications to them should try to connect on a personal level," says B2B copywriter Ken Norkin. "That means starting out by conveying an understanding of the customer's situation and in particular the problem that your product is going to solve. You not only need to present the data but tell your readers what it means to them."

Now, most marketers divide the marketing world into two

segments: business-to-business marketing and business-to-consumer marketing. The "rational" school of B2B marketing says business and consumer are not at all the same. The "emotional" school says that B2B and B2C marketing are more alike than they are different.

But I actually think there is a third segment, real but rarely recognized: hybrid marketing (see our three-circles illustration below). Hybrid markets are those that exhibit characteristics of both business prospects and consumers. Hybrid prospects are consumers who exhibit many of the behaviors shared by business prospects or vice versa.

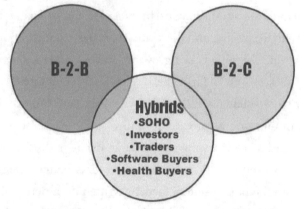

An example of a classic hybrid market is **SOHO**s — small business/home business. These are for the most part self-employed people working at home or a small rented office. Many work alone. Some have a small staff.

Technically, because they are business owners, selling to SOHOs is B2B marketing. But SOHOs often behave more like individual consumers than corporate executives, engineers, or IT professionals.

For a corporate middle manager, the purchase of an expensive color digital printer may indeed be a largely dispassionate decision: one of many tasks she must content with that week.

The SOHO is more likely to agonize over this purchase decision on an emotional level. Reason: The expense of the equipment is much more of a personal issue, as it is coming out of the SOHO's pocket, and he may have to decide between buying the printer versus sending his kid to camp that summer. In addition, the SOHO may cultivate a personal excitement from this purchase (having coveted but never owning office equipment this high-tech or costly before) that the corporate employee may not feel.

Farmers are another hybrid market. The family farm is their legacy and livelihood, and there are few issues more emotionally charged than keeping it as a growing concern and passing it on to the children. Yet, a farm is a business, and therefore farmers are, strictly speaking, a B2B and not a consumer market.

I am unaware of any authoritative study on whether business-to-business marketing (and marketing to hybrid markets that exhibit some B2B characteristics) works better when it is reduces to the bare essential facts or written on a personal and emotional level. So I can only relate what I have found during over four decades as a B2B copywriter. And based on that long experience, here is what I believe works in B2B marketing.

Business-to-business prospects are far less dispassionate about their jobs and industries than is often imagined. For example, I attended a technical seminar years ago where two telecommunications managers both turned red in the face and nearly came to blows in a heated argument about whether TDMA or CDMA was the better platform for wireless communications.*

The business prospect buys not only for his company but for his own personal benefit, and the two are sometimes at odds. Often a prospect will specify a product that may not be the optimum solution for his company's problem if he believes it will personally make his life easier or his employment more secure. This is why for years the maxim in IT was: "No IT manager ever got fired for buying an IBM product that didn't work." Even if another brand had superior features or better price/performance, IBM was the safer choice for IT buyers who answered to senior management. This is why when RCA entered the mainframe market to compete with IBM by offering what some said was a technologically superior machine, they failed: No IT Director wanted to hear from his CEO when the RCA mainframe had problems, "Well, why did you buy a mainframe from a company that makes Victrolas?"

While B2B prospects can be engaged and sold emotionally, once that engagement takes place, B2B prospects require much more rational evidence to support their buying decisions than consumers.

So the answer to our question "Are B2B prospects devoid of emotion?" is decidedly no. On the contrary and, despite what they themselves may say, much of B2B buying is motivated by emotional reasons rather than logical facts.

However, the emotion in B2B marketing, as in consumer, typically comes in the front-end of the sale, which involves atten-

---

*Time Division Multiple Access and Code Division Multiple Access.

tion-getting and engagement. This is the place in the B2B sales cycle where emotion-driven consumer advertising techniques maximize marketing effectiveness. An example is the old TV campaign for Macintosh vs. Microsoft, where Apple computers are positioned as cooler, friendlier, and problem-free. Branding as a factor in making purchase decisions is, as a rule, based much more on emotion than logic. Apple users are often evangelists and fans of all things Apple and their products, while Windows users like me often actively avoid Apple hardware.

Once emotion hooks the B2B prospect, and he begins a serious evaluation of your product, logic, and intellect come into play. He gradually shifts from an emotional buyer (though residue of his emotional reaction to your marketing stays with him throughout the sales cycle) and increasingly toward a rational mode of decision-making.

At this stage, the prospect is performing due diligence. He has to make sure the product can perform the functions required; fits the application's requirements; is compatible with his current infrastructure; has the proper specifications; and can handle the buyer's application. Here is where traditional informational, fact-based, content-rich B2B marketing — data sheets, brochures, white papers, podcasts, videos, and webinars — are most useful to buyers, because they contain answers to the buyer's due-diligence research questions.

EMOTION IS MORE POTENT

Though some may argue whether emotion or reason works better in business-to-business or business-to-consumer marketing, I believe it is axiomatic that in both business and consumer marketing, emotion is a more potent mode of persuasion than logical argument. The old saying about this is true: *people buy based on emotion, then justify their purchase based on facts.*

I think more accurately it is emotion that draws the prospect in and makes the sale. The facts, the logic, the product features and benefits are there mostly to offer proof of the claims made about the product.

Now, you may have noticed that, unlike some direct marketers who state that long copy always outperforms short copy in terms of generating response, I have not stated that as an Axiom, because it is not. The fact is that sometimes long copy works best; other times, short copy works better. I have seen this proven in innumerable tests, so I can say with absolute certainty that "long copy is better than short copy" is not even close to an Axiom.

However, that emotion is more powerful in persuasion than raw facts and data is an axiom. And it is the reason why in so many cases, long copy does in fact do better than short copy: If you are just presenting features and benefits, you can do it in relatively few words; but when you are tapping into the mind and emotions of your prospects, doing so often takes more persuasion and longer copy.

One emotional appeal that prospects find particularly appealing is for marketers to be humble, modest, and honest, especially showing not only how wonderful their product is but also being transparent about its warts. For instance, legendary adman James Webb Young, who started selling fruit by mail around the same time that Harry & David did, tells the story of an apple-growing season where he was nearly ruined.

Violent hail storms bombarded his apple trees with ice pellets, causing bruising and pock marks. He feared massive complaints and returns if he shipped the bruised fruit to his mail-order apple buyers. But if he didn't ship the damaged apples, he would have to refund all the orders, and his mail order business would be ruined.

The apples were damaged only cosmetically. The hail had pockmarked the skin, but this did not affect the flavor or freshness.

Young went ahead and filled his orders with the pockmarked apples, and, in each box shipped, he enclosed a preprinted card that read as follows (I am paraphrasing):

Note the pockmarks on some of these apples. This is proof that they are grown at a high mountain altitude, where the same extreme cold that causes sudden hailstorms also firms the flesh and increases the natural sugars, making the apples even sweeter.

According to Young, not a single order was returned. In fact, when orders came in for next year, many order forms had handwritten notes that said, "Pockmarked apples if available; otherwise, the regular kind."

Young's story proves what experienced marketers know:

Often, by being truthful about your weaknesses and flaws, you can gain substantial credibility with your buyer, increasing loyalty, sales, and customer satisfaction.

Years ago, an industrial pump manufacturer, Blackmer, used the "show your warts" strategy with great success. As a chemical engineer, I can tell you that not all pumps perform equally in all applications. Instead of hiding this fact, Blackmer made it a primary advertising claim.

Their trade ads showed a Yellow Pages ripped out of an industrial buying guide, full of listings for pump manufacturers, including Blackmer; the Blackmer name was circled in pen. The headline of the ad read,

> *There are only certain times you should call Blackmer for a pump. Know when?*

The body copy explained (again, I am paraphrasing),

> *In many applications, Blackmer performs no better or worse than any pumps, and so we are not a particularly advantageous choice.*

But, the ad went on,

> *… for certain applications (viscous fluids, fluids containing abrasives, and a few other situations) Blackmer was proven to outperform all other pumps, and were the logical brand of choice.*

Blackmer closed the ad by offering a free technical manual proving the claim.

My old friend, Jim Alexander, of Alexander Marketing in Grand Rapids, Michigan, created this campaign and told me it worked extremely well.

Another example: James DiGeorgia of 21st Century Publishing was concerned that putting disclaimers and fine print required by regulatory bodies would depress response to his e-mail marketing campaigns promoting his stock market and options trading newsletters. Instead of hiding the disclaimers in fine print, however, he put them in the same size type as the rest of the e-mail promotion. He found, to his surprise, that being up front about the warnings and cautions actually increased response!

The conclusion: *Instead of hiding a weakness, be forthright about it.*

HOW TO BE OPEN AND HONEST

Pick one weakness of your product or company. Talk about it frankly in your marketing. Show why either

> the weakness is not really important, or

> how you have designed your product or service to either overcome, solve, or compensate for the weakness.

A famous TV commercial for Wesson oil showed that when you fried chicken parts, some of the oil was absorbed by the cooking chicken, which is not ideal, as absorption makes fried chicken greasy. In the televised test, chicken was fried in a pan with exactly one cup of Wesson oil. After frying, the oil was poured back into the measuring cup. We saw that yes, a little of the oil was absorbed. But, almost all the oil wasn't — and was poured back, save for one tiny teaspoon. So a perceived negative, oil absorption, is demonstrated as a strong **unique selling proposition (USP)**: when you fry with a cup of Wesson oil, it all comes back except just one teaspoon. So while there is some absorption of the cooking oil by the food, with Wesson it is far less greasy than with other brands.

A similar flaw-based product ad was for a new technologically advanced golf ball design. The ad claimed the engineers had done their aerodynamics too well, and the balls were going farther than intended. Of course, with the average duffer having an anemic drive, this is a product benefit cleverly disguised as a "defect."

In an article in the *Harvard Business Review* (1/26/2015), Michael D. Harris writes about the power of stories to evoke an emotional response.

> *One of the best ways for customers to experience your complex product is by sharing a vivid customer story," says Harris. "Research has shown that stories can activate the region of the brain that processes sights, sounds, tastes, and movements.*

Harris concludes:

> *Rather than thinking of the emotional mind as irrational, think of it this way: an emotion is simply the way the unconscious communicates its decision to the conscious mind.*

For many years, Covenant House, a well-known fundraiser, sent a small paperback book as its direct mail fundraising package. The book was packed with heartbreaking story after story of how poor kids suffered on the streets of New York, and encouraged the reader to make a donation which would go toward helping Covenant House feed and shelter these homeless children.

A direct mail package with a free book enclosed with the mailing is called a "**bookalog**." When Covenant House first started mailing, fundraising professionals were skeptical the package could work, because it costs so much. But the stories had such emotional power that the bookalog package remained a control for many years — and the appeal of this mailer was overwhelmingly emotional and story-based.

BELIEFS, DESIRES, FEELINGS

While emotional appeals are stronger than appeals based on pure logic or fact, they only work if you tap into the right emotions. These are the emotions your prospect has concerning either buying or owning your product, or the problem your product solves.

Although this may be a complex mix of emotions, usually one stands out head and shoulders above all the others. We call this the **dominant resident emotion** — the main thought and feeling that possesses your prospect when evaluating purchase of your product. Top copywriter Clayton Makepeace gave this advice:

Start your copy by entering the conversation the prospect is already having in his or her mind.

And this conversation almost always centers on the dominant resident emotion, which some marketers call the **core buying complex** — the thoughts and feelings that drive the purchase decision.

Importantly, starting with the prospect's emotions, of course, means you are starting with the prospect, not the product. This is in fact something great marketers do that mediocre managers often don't. The merely competent, average marketer studies the product and bases her campaign around the product, in particular, features, benefits, unique selling proposition, price, offer, and so on. She starts with the product, and then describes product information to connect with the prospect.

Beliefs, Desires, Feelings (BDF)

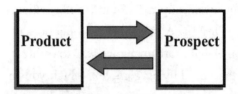

Well, features, benefits, and product differentiation are all important, especially in appealing to the prospect's logical mind. But as the Axiom of Marketing #6 states, *appealing to emotion is more powerful than logical arguments*. So while the merely competent marketer starts with the product (see the BDF illustration) and then moves to connect with the prospect, the master marketer knows and understands this Axiom, and so she starts with the prospect — his needs, wants, fears, concerns, problems, desires, and dominant resident emotion — and then moves to show how the product satisfies these deeply felt needs, wants, and desires.

The **BDF formula** is a methodology for uncovering the prospect's dominant resident emotion or core buying process. It says that the core buying process consists of three components which form the BDF acronym:

> **Belief.** What does the prospect believe, especially on issues centering around your product or offer?
>
> **Desire.** What does the prospect desire and want to obtain?
>
> **Feelings.** What are the dominant and secondary emotions involved with the purchase of this type of product?

What makes the BDF formula quick and easy to use is that

marketers already know most of the answers: You can't be active in a market and product category for any significant length of time without picking up most of this information through observation and testing. All the BDF formula does is examine the data in a somewhat more analytical way to codify it for a clearer picture of the core buying complex, which you then target in your marketing campaigns.

Let's take a look at a quick example or two in each category:

Belief. We know from experience that consumers in certain markets are patriotic; these include coin collectors and gun enthusiasts. We also know that buyers of investment newsletters are mostly older conservative males; and buyers of nutritional supplements and other alternative health offers are distrustful of the pharmaceutical industry, which marketers refer to as "big pharma," believing drug companies care more about profits than making people healthy. Many IT professionals believe that they are smarter than other people and that IT is the most important

Desires. IT professionals desire recognition, praise, ongoing training in the current hot computer platforms to maintain their marketability in the IT job marketplace, and to be left along to do their job without annoying interference from users and management.

Feelings. IT often feels an adversarial relationship with the users and senior management they serve. IT professionals say, "Users don't know what they want, can't communicate their requirements, and when we give them the system, complain that it is not what they asked for." (Users counter: "IT delivers systems late, over budget, and without the functionality and features we asked for.)

The BDF analysis is an effective tool for uncovering the emotional hot buttons of the prospect. And by doing so, it maximizes the effectiveness and response rates to promotions that center on emotional rather than logical appeals as the 8th marketing axiom dictates we should do.

CASE STUDY

A consulting firm specializing in soft skills training for IT sent a mailing to generate leads for an on-site workshop. The name of the seminar was *Interpersonal Skills for IT professionals* and the mailing used that as the headline. It generated a 0.5% response rate.

The marketing department did a BDF analysis of IT professionals and agreed that as far as dominant resident emotion goes, it is adversarial, as noted in the "feelings" bullet above.

Marketing sent out a new mailer (see next page) with a headline based on this dominant resident emotion:

> *Important news for every IT professional who has ever felt like telling a user, "Go to hell…"*

They then split test this new mailer against the original.

Result: a 3% response generating six times the number of leads as the original mailer.

THE
COMMUNICATION WORKSHOP

Important news for every systems professional who has ever felt like telling an end-user, "Go to hell..."

Dear IS Manager:

It's ironic.

Today's users demand to be treated as customers of IS.

Yet many systems professionals don't have the customer service skills to make the relationship work.

Our training program, "Interpersonal Skills for IS Professionals," solves that problem ... by giving IS staff the skills they need to deal effectively with end-users and top management in today's service-oriented corporate environment.

Presented jointly by The Center for Technical Communication and The Communication Workshop -- two leaders in teaching "soft skills" to technical professionals -- "Interpersonal Skills for IS Professionals" quickly brings your team to a new level in listening, negotiating, team work, customer service, and other vital skills for communicating complex systems ideas and technical processes to managers and end users.

Many leading companies ... including IBM, AT&T, Symbol Technologies, Price Waterhouse, Cigna, American Airlines, Lever Brothers, Barnett Technologies, First Union, and Turner Broadcasting ... count on us to help their technical professionals communicate more effectively and work more productively. You can too.

For more information, including an outline of our "Interpersonal Skills for IS Professionals" program, just complete and mail the enclosed reply card. Or call (516) 767-9590. You'll be glad you did.

Sincerely,

Gary Blake, Ph.D., Director

P. S. Reply now and we'll also send you a FREE copy of our new tip sheet, "The IS Professional's Guide to Improving Listening Skills." It will help everyone in your department gain a quicker, more accurate understanding of what users want, while helping to transform your customers from uninitiated "end users" into "educated consumers" who are easier and more reasonable to deal with.

CONCLUSION

In this book, I have presented *The AXIOMS of Marketing*, meaning they hold in all situations, all the time — and not just some or even most of the time.

The problem with me doing so is that, while I can offer ample evidence of these principles holding true over and over again, I cannot prove beyond a shadow of a doubt that they have never failed in any marketing campaign. Again, I believe they have not and cannot, but I am unable to prove that, simply because there are countless marketing campaigns that have been conducted over the years, and I am privy to the actual results of only a tiny fraction of them.

So at best, I am right, and you can put these axioms into practice confidently and safely, knowing they will improve your marketing results each and every time you use them.

At worst, I am wrong about them being axioms, but in that case I know from decades of study, observation, and experience that they hold whenever used.

So, you can still put the AXIOMS of marketing into practice confidently and safely, knowing they will improve your marketing results virtually every time you use them.

Either way, you come out the winner!

RESOURCES

Godin, Seth, *All Marketers Are Liars: The Power of Authentic Stories in a Low-Trust World* (Portfolio, 2005). Godin's book spotlights the important of storytelling in marketing, and explains why a good story can often be a much more effective selling tool than a conventional features-and-benefits presentation.

Cialdini, Robert B., *Influence: The Psychology of Persuasion, Revised Edition* (William Morrow, 1993). A fascinating compilation of numerous psychological experiments and observations designed to show how we are influenced and persuaded by the actions and words of others.

Reiss, Steven, *Who Am I? The 16 Basic Desires That Motivate Our Actions and Define Our Personalities* (Berkley Books, 2005). Reiss argues that all human actions are driven by one or more of 16 basic human desires. These include curiosity, idealism, eating, status, and the desire for acceptance.

Lawrence, Paul and Nohria, Nitin, *Driven: How Human Nature Shapes Our Choices* (Jossey-Bass, 2002). Two Harvard professors claim that all human choices are controlled by four drives: the drive to acquire, to bond, to learn, and to defend.

Underhill, Paco, *Why We Buy: The Science of Shopping* (Simon & Schuster, 1999). This book explores how consumer purchase decisions are influenced and made in retail settings including stores, restaurants, and showrooms – in other words, how and why people shop.

Caskey, Bill, *Same Game New Rules: 23 Timeless Principles for Selling and Negotiating* (Winpointe Publishing, 2005). Caskey has written one of the most sensible, practical books ever written on face-to-face selling, a discipline every marketer should understand, with 23 principles that can quickly make you a more effective salesperson.

Longinotti-Buitoni, Gian Luigi, *Selling Dreams: How to Make Any Product Irresistible* (Simon & Schuster). In this book, the former president of Ferrari North America reveals his secrets for creating an intensive, red-hot desire in consumers to own your product.

Kilbourne, Jean, *Deadly Persuasion: Why Women and Girls Must Fight the Addictive Power of Advertising* (The Free Press, 1999). An activist author, Kilbourne has written an anti-advertising book. But it's packed with examples and case studies of ad campaigns that have been especially successful throughout the years selling products to women.

Ware, Leslie, *Selling It: The Incredible Shrinking Package and Other Marvels of Modern Marketing* (W.W. Norton & Company, 2002). Ware, who was a columnist for Consumer Reports, has written an expose of deceptive and fraudulent advertising, illustrated with dozens of examples. Some are blatant cheats, but many others are instructive – and absolutely fascinating.

Joyner, Mark, *The Irresistible Offer: How to Sell Your Product or Service in 3 Seconds or Less* (John Wiley & Sons, 2005). Reading this book causes you to spend several hours thinking about offers, which is an invaluable exercise every marketer should do.

ABOUT EPERT

ob Bly is a copywriter with over four decades of experience in business-to-business and direct response marketing. McGraw-Hill calls Bob Bly "America's top copywriter."

A professional copywriter since 1982, Bob has written copy for more than 100 clients including AT&T, IBM, Intuit, Agora Publishing, The Motley Fool, Weiss Research, Brooklyn Union Gas, PSE&G, BOC Chemicals, M&T Chemicals, and Prentice Hall.

Bob is the author of more than one hundred books including *The Complete Idiot's Guide to Direct Marketing* (Alpha) and *The Copywriter's Handbook* (Henry Holt).

He has published over 100 articles in numerous periodicals including *New Jersey Monthly*, *Cosmopolitan*, *Successful Meetings*, *City Paper*, and *Science Books and Films*. His e-newsletter, *The Direct Response Letter*, has 35,000 subscribers.

Bob has given presentations on copywriting and marketing for dozens of organizations including the American Marketing Association, Thoroughbred Software, Bull Information Systems, IBM, American Artists and Writers Inc., Society for Technical Communication, and the National Speakers Association.

Bob has been a member of the Business Marketing Associa-

tion, American Institute of Chemical Engineers, and Specialized Information Publishers Association. He has won many writing awards including an IMMY from the Information Industry Association, a Gold Echo from the Direct Marketing Association, Copywriter of the Year from AWAI, Lifetime Achievement in Marketing award from Early to Rise, an Honorable Mention from the New York Book Festival, and a Standard of Excellence award from the Web Marketing Association.

Bob has been featured in major media including the *National Enquirer*, *Nation's Business*, CNBC, CBS *Hard Copy*, the *New York Post*, *Investor's Business Daily*, and *The Writer* plus dozens of radio shows nationwide. He holds a B.S. in chemical engineering from the University of Rochester.

Prior to becoming a freelancer, Bob was a marketing writer for Westinghouse Aerospace and Defense and the advertising manager of Koch Engineering, a manufacturer of chemical process equipment.

He can be reached at:

Bob Bly

Copywriter

31 Cheyenne Drive

Montville, NJ 07045

Phone: 973-263-0562

Fax: 973-263-0613

E-mail: rwbly@bly.com

Web: *www.bly.com*

GET 4 SPECIAL REPORTS!
(A $116 VALUE . . . YOURS FREE!)

Subscribe to my free e-newsletter *The Direct Response Letter* today — *www.bly.com/reports* — and you also get **4 free bonus reports** totaling over 200-pages of actionable how-to marketing content.

TOTAL VALUE: $116

** Free Special Report #1

Make $100,000 a Year Selling Information Online.

** Free Special Report #2

Secrets of Successful Business-to-Business Marketing.

** Free Special Report #3

How to Double Your Response Rates.

** Free Special Report #4

Online Marketing That Works.

Each report has a list price of *$29*.

The total value of this package of reports is **$116**.

But you can get all 4 reports FREE when you click on the link below now . . .

WWW.BLY.COM/REPORTS